'As Christians, we are often told
we ever taught *how* to do them
do these things in the way and ⌐ᵣ
captivated by *Reflex*. This is not a checklist of dos and don'ts but an
invitation to become more like Jesus from the inside out, participat-
ing in the transforming work that Jesus catalyses in the life of every
disciple. This book is a must-read!'

—DOUG PAUL, managing partner, Catapult;
author, *Ready or Not: Kingdom Innovation
for a Brave New World*

'An insightful book, both for our personal walk with Jesus and for a
landscape that has changed for churches worldwide.'

—TRISH MORGAN, worship leader;
singer-songwriter; church planter

'A beautifully written book that can help us all realise something
needs to change: we need to stop and encounter Jesus, so we can be
like him. John has written a gift that can make a difference to each
one of us.'

—REV CRIS ROGERS, rector, All Hallows Bow;
director, Making Disciples; chair,
Spring Harvest Planning Group

'This book should be essential reading for every Christian. As former
senior pastor of Frontline Church, and subsequently as director of
Kairos Connexion, I have had the privilege of watching John emerge
as a brilliant leader. It is a joy to be part of his church and under his
leadership. John lives what he preaches, living life as a reflex to the
grace and love of God, the amazing gospel, the reflex way of living.
The central message of this book is life-transforming and a massive
relief to all who have tried to live the Christian life as a set of rules,
trying to earn God's favour, or trying to impress others. It is liberat-
ing to live life as a reflex. Read this book to learn how to "gospel"
yourself and how to make this way of living true for you too.'

—DR NIC HARDING, director, Kairos Connexion

JOHN HARDING

REFLEX

THE NATURAL WAY TO
LIVE THE CHRISTIAN LIFE

100
MOVEMENTS
PUBLISHING

First published in 2021 by 100 Movements Publishing
www.100Mpublishing.com
Copyright © 2021 by John Harding

www.100Mpublishing.com
www.movementleaderscollective.com
www.catalysechange.org

ISBN: 978-1-955142-99-1 (paperback)

Cover design and interior design by Revo Creative Ltd

For bulk orders, email admin@frontline.org.uk

100 Movements Publishing
An imprint of Movement Leaders Collective
Cody, Wyoming

To all those who from time to time have become weary in following Jesus. May the words you read help you to recapture the joy of your salvation.

Reflex
re·flex | \ 'rē -, fleks

An automatic and often inborn response to a stimulus
that typically involves a nerve impulse passing inward
from a receptor to the spinal cord and then passing
outward from the spinal cord to an effector (such as a
muscle or gland) without reaching the level of
consciousness and often without passing
to the brain.
MERRIAM-WEBSTER DICTIONARY

Or put more simply …

An action performed unconsciously as a result of a stimulus.
JOHN HARDING

CONTENTS

FOREWORD

GAVIN CALVER

Many Christians live with the relentless pressure to do more. The activism that has driven so much of evangelical Christianity has, at times, been wonderful, but it has also meant we often overestimate our activities and underestimate our King! *Reflex* challenges us to a greater depth of relationship with Jesus in the most natural of ways. We don't have to keep trying to do more. Instead, we can come to him just as we are – bringing our tiredness and our burdens – and allow fruitfulness to flow from intimacy with Jesus. Sound good?

Well, this is a good-news book, centred around the gospel, and it's evident that this good news has changed the author's life. It's a good-news message that is fresh in John each day and not only drives him but is central to his wonderful church. John is the real deal. And he's not afraid to admit he's not the finished article. His commitment on the ground, as well as his humility and authenticity, make him a leader I hugely admire. John's love for Scripture and his living relationship with Jesus pour out on every page of this book.

Reflex will take you on a journey of reflection and discovery. I strongly encourage you not to rush through it. Answer the questions honestly, take your time and pause throughout the book to reflect and pray. In today's busy and distracted world, we need to make space for encountering Jesus. An old mentor once said to me, 'Never love the work of the Lord more than the Lord of the work.' It's time to live the kind of

Christianity that this book speaks of. It's time to move away from striving in our own strength, and instead live a life that daily experiences the grace of God, a grace which empowers us to be true disciples.

As we pursue Jesus and get to know him better, we will live a life that increasingly reflexes in the right way at every opportunity. Our world needs us to look more like Jesus, and this wonderful book will help us get things back in the right order and perspective.

Enjoy the adventure!

INTRODUCTION

THE PROBLEM

There is no doubt that the modern world is exhausting.

We feel worn out. Weary. We live life at a frantic pace. Constant online connection fuels comparison and competition. We push ourselves to do more, achieve more, *be* more.

And it's taking its toll on us.

Studies in the UK show that anxiety has trebled in young people aged eighteen to twenty-four.[1] Three quarters of our eight- to sixteen-year-olds are worried about climate change, with another 22 per cent 'very worried'.[2] We might call it an *anxiety explosion.* We are worried. Worried about missing out.[3] Worried about not achieving our full potential. Worried about our kids. Worried about our health. Worried about our planet. Worried about the economy. Worried about the future. Worried about worrying too much (or too little).

If you are a follower of Jesus, maybe if you and I were to sit down and have a frank conversation over coffee, if together we were to scratch beneath the veneer, we might find we too carry deep worries and fears. A fear that we are not quite making the grade. A worry that we are somehow letting God down ... letting the world down. Perhaps this expresses itself in the drive to be better, or even be the best ... to achieve the dizzying heights of Christian superstar status. Maybe this gap, this space between how things *are* and how we feel things *ought to be* makes us feel rubbish, like giving up.

Maybe you are on the ascent, really going places. Smashing it. If you keep going at this rate, one day they will even write a book about you and your achievements. Or maybe 'the ascent' once described you, and then you hit burnout, and now you are trying to figure out what it means to live in the descent, in the ashes of a broken life. Perhaps the pressures of church and the Christian life have put you on the verge of abandoning the Christian life all together, because it is too hard, requires too much effort and brings little immediate reward.

Surely this isn't what the Christian life should be?

So where did it all go wrong?

Could it be that as followers of Jesus we have been duped into exchanging the joyful freedom of walking with Jesus for a corporate, performance-driven culture? Could it be we've swapped the natural way to live the Christian life with a way of living that feels forced and inauthentic? Could it be that our faith has become a box-ticking exercise?

Could it be that the church, called to model real life to the world, has somehow lost its way? Could it be that the church, called to be distinctive, like salt and light, has gradually become transformed into the image of a world it was called to transform?

But what if living the Christian life could be like a reflex – as natural as blinking when poked in the eye?

The Obsession with Measuring Outcomes

For over a decade I was a schoolteacher. I taught Religious Studies in both secular state schools and church schools. I taught challenging pupils, and I taught bright and ambitious pupils. I *loved* it.

I loved 'moulding minds', as we used to say, somewhat humorously. I loved living day by day with non-Christians, modelling the joyful freedom of a relationship with Jesus to both staff and students. And I knew God's favour and blessing in those places.

But there was something I didn't love about teaching. One thing all teachers fear.

OFSTED. The national body of school inspectors.

Now don't get me wrong, I wasn't fearful of the inspectors. The way I saw it – as a rather ambitious and competitive young man – inspection was simply a chance to show off and have the experts sing my praises. It was like painting by numbers: you just had to get their checklist-criteria, build a lesson around it, and *voila*, you got the top grade.

Neither am I saying that inspectors are bad people, prowling like wolves for underperforming teachers – although I have met the occasional clipboard-carrying school inspector with that sort of vibe.

But what really frustrated me about the inspection system was that it created a culture within schools that was all about *outcomes*. It was all about the results. Schools became obsessed with measuring things. What percentage of pupils achieved a pass? What percentage of pupils from a minority ethnic background passed? How many pupils with special educational needs achieved the highest grades? How did the results in one class compare with another? How well did pupils progress from course entry to completion? We spent inordinate amounts of time focused on data analysis – producing graphs and charts – rather than planning engaging lessons and caring for pupils.

My success or failure as a teacher was based entirely on the measurement of the outcomes of my pupils. Our school system here in England still currently ranks schools according to this data. Schools are put into league tables much like football teams. Each year it's possible to find out how 'successful' one school is compared with another school down the road.

Of course, OFSTED inspection plays an important role in education. Accountability is important. But the problem with the system is that teachers, schools and local authorities often make decisions based on how to get better outcomes. Teachers end up 'teaching to the test' rather than allowing the curiosity and interest of the pupils to grow and develop in a way that helps them engage holistically with the world around them. There is not time to go off-topic, to respond to what pupils have personally seen or experienced. Why? Because the exam deadlines are looming. Schools invariably cut or reduce the curriculum subjects that are not being measured. After all, if it is not measured it is not important. So the amount of time spent enjoying music, art and sport is reduced.

Rant over, let me get to the point, which is simply this: any good teacher instinctively knows that input is more important than outcomes. An experienced, seasoned teacher knows that if you spend your time and energy inputting the right stuff, the outcomes take care of themselves. Input the right stuff into the spiritual, social, emotional, physical and intellectual needs of a child, and they will naturally achieve the best outcomes. You might even call it a *reflex*.

And, actually, we know that this way of prioritising and obsessing over outcomes is counter-productive. It can do more harm than good. When inspections are looming, the pressure on teachers filters down to pupils and creates negative learning environments. Indeed, some teachers would argue that teaching aimed at ticking the boxes of an up-and-coming inspection can negatively impact pupil grades. Why? The school gets so focused on hitting the right outcomes, and evidencing the outcomes that have already taken place, that they neglect the inputs. After all, we all have a limited amount of time in the day, so when the pressure is on to demonstrate what has already taken place, teachers may well invest less time and energy into what is currently happening.

Likewise, when a hospital is focused on clearing beds and hitting the targets of seeing the right number of patients per hour, the results can be deadly. When a church majors on the numbers of 'bums on seats' or the amount of money given, their whole approach becomes skewed. This is because growth and giving are natural outcomes of the right sorts of stimuli. Give the right sort of medical care, and the beds will clear. Get the inputs right, and the rest seems to take care of itself.

I imagine if you work as a doctor or nurse, a social worker or in business, you can apply all I've just said about schools to your own context. From what I understand, a similar culture exists for those delivering Uber Eats and order picking for Amazon. We have created (or cooperated with the creation of) a world obsessed with measuring, grading and outcomes ... a performance-driven culture. And in doing so, we take our eyes off what really matters: the quality of the input.

As the farmers of Yorkshire used to say, 'A pig never got fatter by weighing it.'

We see it in parenting. The anxious, frazzled parent who measures their kid's performance against the rest of the pack.

In some circles it expresses itself in competitive conversation over the post-drop-off coffee.

'My boy is reading books for eleven-year-olds, and he's only three.'

'Well, my darling daughter has been chosen to swim for the county.'

'Ours do gymnastics Mondays and Wednesdays, orchestra Tuesdays and Thursdays, football Saturdays and Sundays, *and* they have extra lessons before breakfast each day.'

One-upmanship.

If your kid has been to Tenerife, their little darling has been to *Elevenerife*. No wonder our children are so stressed, so anxious, so fearful of failure. Their outcomes are constantly measured. Their achievements celebrated through the boast post.

And we see it in the church: the Christian life reduced to a tick-list of achievements.

Pray. Tick.

Read Bible. Tick.

Tithe. Tick.

Hand out gospel tract or flyer for evangelistic event. Tick.

In other words, we have turned the joyful freedom of the gospel into religious practice.

I grew up in the church. A great church. Many people in that Christian community showed an interest in me and invested in me. We sung our songs of worship with enthusiasm. The Bible was the basis for all that was preached. But somewhere along the way, what I heard and experienced made me feel like a failure. I went to Bible College – and loved it and met my wife there – but this gnawing sense of not quite being good enough continued to grow. I am sure my feelings of inadequacy were far more to do with my filters than anything that was preached or communicated, but what I heard was:

You need to do more.
You need to pray more.
You need to read your Bible more.
You need to give more.
You need to serve more.
You need to tell more people about Jesus.
That stuff you do, it is just not enough.

I heard the words of Jesus in Luke 12:48, 'From everyone who has been given much, much will be demanded' and felt a burden to give more back to God through my self-effort.

More, more, more.

Somewhere along the way, we have lost sight of the gospel. We have taken the good news of grace, the good news of what God has already done for us on the cross, and exchanged it for performance-based religion, a Christianity based on *our* efforts and *our* achievements.

We have made it into a religion, because that is how religion operates. Religion is all about achieving the right outcomes. If you want God to accept you, if you want God to love you, if you want God to bless you, if you want God to give you eternal life in paradise, you better make the grade. You better pass the exam.

Religion, whether that be Islam and its Five Pillars or Judaism and its Ten Commandments and 613 *mitzvahs*, is about the *oughts* and *musts* and *shoulds*. It is about the *ought nots* and the *must nots* and the *should nots*. It is about earning. It is about making the grade, getting the right outcome.

And it's such an exhausting way to live.

A Uniquely Different Gospel

It is into this sort of religious human experience that Jesus speaks these words of life:

> Are you tired? Worn out? Burned out on religion? Come to me. Get away with me and you'll recover your life. I'll show you how to take a real rest. Walk with me and work with me – watch how I do it. Learn the unforced rhythms of grace. I won't lay anything heavy or ill-fitting on you. Keep company with me and you'll learn to live freely and lightly.
>
> Matthew 11:28–30 MSG

That sounds like good news indeed. It sounds like the gospel. It sounds like what I signed up for.

Christ calls us to come to him in our weariness, to bring our burdens to him and to find rest in him.

These words from Matthew's Gospel speak life and lightness to our hearts. To understand them we have to understand a bit about the life of a Jewish rabbi (a religious teacher). We have to understand some of the religious clothing and fashion of Jesus' day. A good Jew at the time of Jesus would wear an item of clothing like a shawl or scarf called a tallit. A tallit is a prayer shawl, usually white with blue threads running through. If you were to go to the Western Wall in Jerusalem today, you would see devoted Jews praying with their tallits lifted up to cover their heads. Likewise, enter any synagogue, and you will see Jews wearing their tallits as the Torah scroll is read.

The tallit has fringes, like tassels (Hebrew *tzitzit*). These threads run through the fabric, and in total there are 613 threads: one for each of the Old Testament commandments. Putting your tallit on was a symbolic act of showing that you were under the weight of the commands or, in Hebrew, *the mitzvahs.* In fact, in some more recent Jewish traditions a boy or a girl puts on their tallit for the first time at their *bar/ bat mitzvah*, becoming literally a 'son/daughter of the commandments'. It signifies that they are now under the weight of fulfilling all the commands. A heavy burden to bear indeed.

There are 248 positive commands *to do* something and 365 negative *do nots* (maybe one for each day of the year!). So, for example, one thread running through the tallit would represent the command to circumcise baby boys, another to remind you to leave a corner of your field unreaped for the poor. And so on and so forth.

Jesus undoubtedly wore a tallit. When the haemorrhaging woman touched the hem of Jesus' garment, she was most probably touching the tassels on his tallit.[4] When Jesus called out to Jairus' daughter, he spoke to her lifeless corpse *'Talitha koum'*, most likely meaning *arise to my tallit.*[5] In a sense, Jesus was fulfilling Jewish messianic prophecy and expectation, for it was believed that the Messiah would rise with healing in his wings, symbolised by the outstretched tallit.[6] Imagine a shawl held in outstretched arms, rising over the head.

And Jesus, like all rabbis, would interpret the laws. Rabbis would put their own spin on how to follow the 613 commandments. So for example, one of the *mitzvahs* was to tithe, but rabbis debated what exactly should be tithed. Of what exactly should you give 10 per cent? In Matthew 23, Jesus is aware of this debate. Some rabbis taught you had to tithe all your crops and spices, including dill, cumin and mint; others felt mint was nothing more than a weed, so you didn't need to tithe 10 per cent of it. One *mitzvah* stated you could not plough a field on a Sabbath. Some rabbis interpreted this to mean you could not even move a chair, in case you accidentally ploughed up the ground beneath the chair leg. Each rabbi had his own interpretation of the laws. There were varying degrees of rigidity depending on the rabbinical school of thought.

Can you see how heavy religion can be? How outcome-focused it is? How box-ticking?

Now the teachings of each rabbi, symbolised by his tallit, were known as his *yoke*.[7] The rabbi's yoke was his interpretation of how to follow the laws. The idea that a tallit was like a yoke came from the image that the tallit sat on your shoulders like a yoke that sat on the shoulders of two cows or oxen, binding them together to plough the field. When you chose to follow a particular rabbi, you came under their yoke, their interpretation of the laws. It detailed the extent of your religious duty or work.

And along comes Rabbi Jesus and says, if you are weary with that way of living, if you are burned out with religion, come to me. Take my tallit, my yoke upon you. It is light. It is easy. It is natural. It is not about rules and regulations. It is not about performance and outcomes. It is about *relationship*.

Come to me. Come to me and find rest.

Follower of Jesus, what if it were that simple? What if many of the things we are trying to do to be good Christians were more like natural outcomes to the input of intimacy, rather than the goal in and of itself?

This is not a book about all the things you need to *do* to get better. It is not a self-help book. It is a good-news book. It is a call to the weary to receive and enjoy and apply what has already been done for us, the helpless. It is about discovering, or rediscovering, a Jesus-patterned way of living. It is about learning how to receive from Jesus; receiving the right sorts of inputs that will naturally reflex with the right sorts of outcomes. It is about how inputting the gospel and taking on the yoke of Jesus leads us into a more natural way of living out his kingdom mandate. All those outcomes – all those promises of God working within us to transform us, and through us to transform the world around us – need no longer feel like goals or tasks to be achieved.

We are going to tear up our spiritual to-do list, and begin to trust Jesus that these things will naturally flow out of his good news, alive and at work within us.

A reflex.

What if living the Christian life could be as natural as blinking when poked in the eye?

QUESTIONS FOR DISCUSSION

1. By what 'outcomes' do you feel measured – by yourself, God or others?

2. What standard do you feel you're being measured against, and what is the impact of that?

3. In what ways can you relate to the first line of the passage in Matthew 11:28? 'Are you tired? Worn out? Burned out on religion?'

PART I

LAYING
FOUNDATIONS

1

THE REFLEX

*Stimulus or input leads to an automatic
outcome or response.*

When something pokes you in the eye, you blink. Get the input right, the outcome naturally follows.

In the same way, many of the things we as Christians strive so hard to achieve are actually more like *outcomes* to the right sort of *input*.

I call this *the reflex principle*.

To understand the reflex principle you have to understand a bit about how the human body works. A reflex is an automatic response to a stimulus. It is a loop of information and response. So, for example, if you take a torch and shine the light into someone's eye, the pupil gets smaller to reduce the amount of light entering the eye. When you move the light away, the pupil gets larger to allow in more light. The light from the torch is the *stimulus*. A message is sent to the brain via the nerves; it is processed, and then sent back to the little muscles that contract and change the shape of the pupil. It happens automatically. It is incredibly precise, constantly adjusting to allow just the right amount of light into the eye for optimal vision. This particular reflex is known as the pupillary light reflex.

Another famous reflex is the knee-jerk reflex (the patellar reflex). You have probably seen it, or even had it performed on you. A doctor will tap just under the knee with a special hammer, and the foot will swing forward. It is automatic (providing you are relaxed and your foot is off the floor). Nerve endings in the knee send a signal to the spinal cord, which sends a message back to the muscles in the leg to move. Again, it is an automatic response to a stimulus. A reflex.

The fact the body works like this is amazing and extremely important. There are many reflexes in the human body. Some are so primitive and develop so early in our lives that we see them in newborn babies, such as the sucking reflex or the gag reflex. Some types of reflex signals travel to the brain or spinal cord and back at something like 266 mph! Of course, this book is not about human biology; it is about our relationship with God, and the impact and response that reflexes out of our encounter with him. For example, perhaps as you consider the complexity and majesty of creation you too may experience a reflex: worship. The *stimulus* is creation. The automatic *response* is to say 'wow' and to worship.

Whenever we see someone we love – a friend, a spouse or a child – a reflex occurs. Feel-good hormones known as oxytocin and dopamine flood the brain. Adrenaline makes the heart beat more rapidly. The pupils dilate. The cheeks may flush. Our palms sweat. These are all physical, automatic responses to the stimulus of seeing a loved one. We call the feeling *love*. A biologist may call it a *reflex*!

Now, as a preacher I have used this metaphor of reflex many times – in the UK, across Europe, Africa, India, South East Asia. Everyone gets it. And when I ask the question, 'What would it mean if there was no physical response to the stimulus?' the answer is always the same. People shout out, 'They'd be dead!' And they are right. It would either mean that the person was dead or very seriously ill indeed, perhaps heavily under the influence of drugs. That is why reflexes are tested when a person is admitted to hospital as an emergency. Later in this book, we will think about how the reflex principle can be used as a diagnostic tool for spiritual health. But for now, I want us just to focus on this one simple idea.

Stimulus or *input* leads to automatic *outcome* or *response*.

The Power of Metaphor

I know that the word *reflex* is not in the Bible. I know that. Neither are the words *Trinity* or *incarnation*, yet we use these words to describe concepts we see throughout the Bible. They are like short-hand: a simple way of expressing a profound idea. That is how I use the word *reflex*. Reflex is a picture, an idea, a concept to help us take hold of a deeper truth. The more I read through Scripture, the more I see that there are certain things we are called to input into our lives. There are good stimuli. And there are certain things that happen when we input those things: we reflex with an outcome. Indeed, one of the starting points for writing this book was simply to thumb through my Bible, cover to cover, and note the multiple places I had penned the word *reflex* in the margin over the years. The more I reflect on how we live the Christian life, the more convinced I am that if we make certain outcomes the aim, or the goal, it just does not work. We get ourselves into all sorts of problems.

But focus on the right inputs, and the outcomes take care of themselves.

The Bible does give us some language to describe the concept of reflex. It is the idea of bearing fruit. In John 15, we have this wonderful passage about how to really live. It is well worth a read. In fact, why not read it right now? I encourage you to read the whole of this book with your Bible open. Don't gloss over or glance at the Bible verses. Read them. They are the best bits of this book! So, turn to John 15 and spend a few minutes soaking in verses 1 to 17.

As you have just seen in John 15, Jesus is the Vine. We are the branches. Jesus is the source of life. As we remain or abide in him, the natural outcome is to bear fruit. This fruit is clearly to do with our works, how we *do* the Christian life, because Jesus states that apart from him we can *do* nothing. So, all the things we think we need to do as Christians – our witness, our giving, our serving, our loving, among many other things – are more like bearing fruit. It is as natural as an apple tree producing apples. We don't find an apple tree desperately and frantically trying to squeeze out another apple. With the right sort of care and the inputs of light, water and nutrition, the harvest comes. In the same way, the fruit we bear as Christians is a natural, organic, in-built response to the right sort of conditions. In other words, as we come to Jesus and abide in him, as we cultivate intimacy with him and rest in his love, we naturally transform the world around us. Right input, right outcome. A reflex.

Another word the Bible uses that captures the idea of a reflex is the word *overflow*. Picture a jug or a vessel being filled until its contents spill out, saturating and impacting its surroundings. The jug overflows. That is input and outcome. Similarly, as we come to Jesus and drink (input), streams of living waters flow out of us (outcome).[1] God is the one who fills our cup in the presence of our enemies until it overflows.[2] Perhaps the imagery here is that as we rest, abide and feast at his table (even in the presence of our enemies) we receive such abundant blessing that it overflows, impacts and transforms our surroundings, and, dare I say, even our enemies?

As God fills us with hope, we overflow and that hope goes into the lives of others. Romans 15:13 says, 'May the God of hope fill you with all joy and peace as you trust in him, so that you may overflow with hope by the power of the Holy Spirit.' Overflowing hope. Ever spent time with someone full of hope? It is contagious. Their hope spills over into our hearts.

This is the same as the reflex principle. As the Father pours his hope into us, that hope fills us up and overflows out from us into the lives of others. The idea of a reflex is just another metaphor, like *fruit-bearing* or *overflowing*. Metaphors help us to see afresh what is already there, and help us process truth that we may never have really understood before. When someone expresses that they don't understand something, we might say, 'It's a bit like this …'. We use metaphor. We create metaphors to help people understand difficult and abstract concepts. Jesus was an expert in this: 'The kingdom of heaven is like … a farmer, a seed, a treasure …'.[3] Metaphors help us understand profound concepts, and they challenge our preconceptions. In fact, the hugely influence scholar Thomas Aquinas argued that all of what we read of God and say of God has to be metaphor. Anything else would minimise and lessen God. For Aquinas, the metaphor was the message.[4]

Now apply the power of the reflex metaphor to a tricky passage like James 2:14–26. In this passage, James talks about the relationship between faith and works. In verse 17, he says, 'faith by itself, if it is not accompanied by action, is dead'. And in verse 21, he notes that Abraham was 'considered righteous for what he did'. One might be forgiven for thinking that James was saying something contradictory to Paul's message of grace;[5] that instead of grace it is somehow our works that save us. Indeed, the mighty sixteenth-century reformer Martin Luther felt James was incompatible with the grace Paul outlines in the epistle to the Romans and called the epistle of James an 'Epistle of Straw' lacking 'gospel'. But when we see works as a *reflex* to faith, it all starts to harmonise. It echoes the idea of bearing fruit as a reflex to abiding. For the person with faith, good deeds, such as meeting the physical needs of the poor (James 2:16), are not a way to earn salvation, but instead are a natural response to our salvation. Through this passage, James uses the Greek word *horate* from the root of *what is seen*. (The NIV translates it as *considered*.) Abraham was *seen to be righteous* by what he did (verse 21). Rahab the prostitute was *seen to be righteous* by what she did (verse 25). I don't believe James is saying that works '*save* us' but rather that works '*show* us'. It is the metaphor of the reflex. The swing of the knee, the blink of the eye – these *show* the doctor testing the reflex that the person is not dead. Good works reflex from the stimulus of saving faith. Works show us we are not spiritually dead (James 1:26).

Now I'm sure there is more to it than that. But for me, this is an example of how the reflex metaphor has opened up a deeper understanding of Scripture.

The Stimulus

So, you might be asking, 'What is *the* stimulus?' Or 'What are the stimuli?' And 'What are the natural outcomes?'

These may well be some of the most powerful questions we could ever ask. They are questions that have led me over the years into much searching of the Scriptures. They are questions I have brought before the Lord in prayer many, many times. They are questions I have spent much time discussing with friends and mentors. For me, these questions have become important enough to finally put pen to paper. Over the next few pages and chapters, we will think about the outcomes that are reflex responses to the right sorts of stimuli. We'll look at holiness, generosity, loving others, serving others, to name but a few – all the kinds of things I was told as a Christian to do more of. The stuff I tried so hard to do and achieve as a young Christian, which ultimately left me feeling weary and overwhelmed by failure. Why? Simply because I had not realised that they were outcomes to the right sort of input.

So, let's start instead by looking at the stimuli. What things, if we input them, will result in the natural outcomes we desire?

As I've explored Scripture and reflected on my own discipleship journey, I initially thought there were multiple stimuli. In the same way that light stimulates the reflex of the eye, or sound stimulates the reflex of the ear, or smell sends a signal to the brain to automatically get you salivating as the aromas of a roast dinner waft out of the kitchen and into your nostrils … I used to think that perhaps there were multiple spiritual inputs. If you wanted to naturally reflex with generosity, you needed the stimulus of thanksgiving. If you wanted to naturally reflex with love for others, you needed to experience the stimulus of the love of God filling your heart.

Well sort of.

But over the years I found that one term more than any other encapsulates all the stimuli of Scripture with great simplicity and beauty, and it is this …

The gospel.

This is the 'good news' that God the Father sent Jesus to live for us, to die for us, and to be resurrected to new life for us, so that we too might be raised from death to eternal life. As Jesus proclaimed in Mark 1, it's the good news that the kingdom of God has come near. Jesus brought news that, as the Messiah, he had come to bring salvation, and God's kingdom had come to bring complete transformation. Heaven was coming to earth, to make all things new. And how was this good news to be taken hold of? As a gift – freely offered and received, not an outcome worked towards or a grade to be achieved. As Ephesians 2:8–9 says, 'For it is by grace you have been saved, through faith – and this is not from yourselves, it is the gift of God – not by works, so that no one can boast.'

The gospel message is that we are saved by *grace*. The word grace means *gift*, or *underserved, unmerited favour*. We couldn't earn it, we don't deserve it, but by faith we receive it.

The gospel message is that this same God is at work through us, his transformed people, bringing about transformation in the world, making earth more and more like heaven – all by his grace.

The gospel is the greatest stimulus we could input into our lives. As we input the gospel, like light penetrating the eye, we reflex with the most remarkable actions and outcomes. The great Baptist preacher Charles Spurgeon put it this way:

Oh, the power, the melting, conquering, transforming power of that dear cross of Christ! ... we have but constantly to tell abroad the matchless story, and we may expect to see the most remarkable spiritual results. ... the most flinty heart will be broken; and with such a fire as the sweet love of Christ, the most mighty iceberg will be melted. ... if we can but find occasion to bring the doctrine of Christ crucified into contact with their natures, it will yet change them, and Christ will be their king.[6]

Bring the message of the cross into contact with your human nature, proclaim the matchless story to your soul, and you will see the most remarkable results.

It will change you.

QUESTIONS FOR DISCUSSION

1. Does following Jesus feel to you more like a reflex or more like a list of outcomes you are trying to achieve?

2. How does the reflex principle make you think about your walk with Jesus in a different way?

3. How does the metaphor of the reflex help you to understand the biblical concepts of grace, faith and works?

2

THE STIMULUS

The gospel brings hope that God is at work to
redeem and restore his broken creation.

So, what do I mean by *gospel input* or *gospel stimulus*? And
what do I mean by *the gospel*?

One of the things I love about the gospel is that it is so
simple a child can grasp it and respond, and yet so deep and
profound that we can spend the rest of our lives trying to work
it out, exploring every facet and nuance. In that respect we
might call the gospel *simplex*, simultaneously and paradoxically simple *and* complex.

I remember hearing the gospel in a Sunday school class
as a six-year-old. For some reason, the class was being held
in the assembly hall of the local junior school I attended. I
wasn't sure why. We sang a song … I don't quite remember
the song, but one of the lines was about thanking the Lord for
my fuzzy wuzzy hair (if I was a bear!). And then a lady who I
didn't really know asked if we would like to receive Jesus into

our hearts, and ask for his forgiveness. I knew right there and then it was what I wanted. I feel joyfully tearful thinking about it even now, thirty-six years later. I have very few early memories. But I remember that moment. I remember it vividly. I knew from that moment I belonged to Jesus. That he had given his life for me. And that I would spend eternity with him. The gospel is wonderfully simple.

A good friend of mine, Dave Sharples, part of our church family and my wider leadership team, has spent over two decades reaching out to inner-city kids. In fact, he was awarded an MBE for his work. He captured the simplicity of the gospel in four simple symbols.

[1]

God loves me.
I have sinned.
Jesus died for me.
I need to decide to live for God.

THE4POINTS have now gone global. I have personally had the privilege of using them to share the gospel with orphan children in Indian slums, militia on the Congolese border, devoted Jews at the Wailing Wall, and drunken clubbers in the early hours in Liverpool's city centre. Over 2,000 years on, and the simple gospel still works. It has not lost an ounce of its power. It still saves sinners. It still transforms lives right across the globe.

And yet, the gospel is also so deep, so profound that over thirty years after making my initial decision to follow Jesus, it still blows me away. It still arrests my attention, causes me to pause and say, 'Wow! Thank you, Jesus!' It still excites me.

Undoubtedly the gospel is a mystery. There is something about it that does not make sense. Something about it that is hard to believe. Beyond human comprehension. The message that someone *like him*, could do something *like that*, for someone *like me* … I can't quite get my head around it. A stumbling block to the wise. Foolishness to the religious. Such is the message of the cross.[2]

For me, the gospel is a bit like my car. I don't have to understand how it works in order for it to work and get me to where I need to be. I just enjoy it. Likewise, the gospel is so simple, and yet so profound, so mysterious, so richly complex, that we don't, and can't, understand everything about it. Instead, we can rest in it. Enjoy it. Let it take us on a journey.

This mysterious nature of the gospel extends to more than a personal and inward transaction between an individual and God. Somehow, through the cumulative transformation of individuals, God's kingdom is being established on earth, right now. Like us, our world is being transformed as a result of the work of Jesus on the cross.

Proclaiming Good News

We can understand this better when we look at the context Jesus came into and the importance of the gospel being *good news*. The gospel is news. Something to be proclaimed. Something to be broadcast. A message to be heard. The word for gospel used in the New Testament is *euangelion;* the prefix *eu* meaning *good* or *beautiful*, and the word *angelos* or *angelion* meaning *messenger* (or indeed *angel*). It made its way into our

English language from the old English *godspell*, meaning *glad tidings*. So, at its heart, the gospel is an announcement.

N. T. Wright captures this brilliantly in his explanation of Romans 1:16 and 1 Thessalonians 2:13:

> The idea of 'good news', for which an older English word is 'gospel', had two principal meanings for first-century Jews. First, with roots in Isaiah, it means the news of YHWH's long-awaited victory over evil and rescue of his people. Second, it was used in the Roman world of the accession, or birthday, of the emperor. Since for Jesus and Paul the announcement of God's inbreaking kingdom was both the fulfilment of prophecy and a challenge to the world's present rulers, 'gospel' became an important shorthand for both the message of Jesus himself, and the apostolic message about him. Paul saw this message as itself the vehicle of God's saving power.[3]

The gospel has been, and always will be, something to be proclaimed.

And what was Jesus proclaiming? What was the good news he embodied in his coming?

Well, this good news proclamation is two-fold: first, it is a message of hope for inward and personal salvation and transformation, like the message I responded to at the age of six, and the message of THE4POINTS. It's the good news that we can enter into relationship with God, a *gospel of salvation*. But second, it is the good news message that, together, we can continue the original commission given to Adam and Eve in the garden to 'fill the earth and subdue it' (Genesis 1:28). We don't just get to heaven; we can bring heaven to earth in the here and now. This *gospel of the kingdom* brings hope that God himself is at work, in ways we can't even imagine, to redeem and restore his broken creation. This proclaims to all of groaning creation that one day it will be made new, 'liberated from its bondage to decay and brought into the freedom and glory of the children of God' (Romans 8:21–22). The two-fold gospel is truly a message proclaimed throughout the Bible – from Genesis to Revelation!

It occurs to me that many Christians reduce the gospel message to something that should only be communicated or preached to those new to the faith. It has become a bit like a hoop we jump through before getting to the 'good stuff', such as eschatology, soteriology and ecclesiology. Once we make that first decision to become a follower of Jesus, we assume we leave the gospel behind and start to focus on the 'deeper stuff'.

The gospel *is* indeed a message that those who don't know Jesus need to hear. But it's not *just* for them. If we reduce the gospel to something that should only be communicated or preached to one group of people, we miss out on its power and relevance to every moment, every person and every sphere of our lives. We end up exchanging the joyful freedom of following Jesus with dry dutiful religion. Could it be that this is at least in part why we end up so weary and disappointed with our faith? Because we have *outgrown* the message of the gospel? Because it is gathering dust in the recesses of our distant memories, and we no longer proclaim it to our souls?

I think so. Certainly, that has been my own experience. When we stop inputting the gospel into our lives, we can subtly slip into performance-based religion, self-effort, striving. If we remove the gospel message from the Scriptures – the

gospel that is evident from Genesis through to Revelation –
then what we are left with is a book of good advice. A self-help
guide. A rule book. Generic religious literature.

So not only is the gospel good news to those who have
never heard it before, and not only is it something to proclaim
and broadcast and make a noise about in the world around us,
it is also good news we need to remind ourselves of. A message that we input. A daily stimulus. News we need to preach
to ourselves.

Preaching to Yourself

The idea of *preaching to yourself* is not new; we see it in the Old
Testament. The psalmist preaches to himself, 'Why, my soul, are
you downcast? Why so disturbed within me? Put your hope in
God, for I will yet praise him, my Saviour and my God' (Psalm
42:5). He reminds himself to, 'Praise the LORD, my soul, and forget not his benefits' (Psalm 103:2). The writer of Lamentations
does likewise, 'Yet this I call to mind and therefore I have hope:
Because of the LORD's great love we are not consumed, for his
compassions never fail' (Lamentations 3:21–22).

The Bible affirms the idea of preaching truth to oneself.
It is an incredibly powerful way of overcoming unhelpful
thought patterns and renewing our minds. Indeed, this was
the essence of Jesus' preaching. Jesus travelled throughout the
region of Galilee, 'proclaiming the good news of God. "The
time has come," he said. "The kingdom of God has come near.
Repent and believe the good news!"' (Mark 1:14–15). *Repent* is
the Greek word *metanoia*, which essentially means to change
how we think. And so, to preach truth to our souls is essentially to participate in the practice and process Jesus called

his first disciples to engage in: a change of mind; a rejection of what is not true; and an embracing or believing of what is true. So, rather than somehow trying to think our way out of unhelpful thoughts, we can proclaim truth aloud. I don't know about you, but there have been times when I've been laid awake in the early hours of the morning, with thoughts racing through my mind, where I have actually had to get up and speak truth out loud in order to still the raging storm within me. I have had to proclaim truth to my soul.

I like how Jerry Bridges in his book *The Discipline of Grace* puts it. He says that we can learn a multitude of disciplines and strategies for godly living, but, 'none [are] more important than learning to preach the gospel to yourself every day'.[4] For Bridges, the key to living the Christian life is to preach the gospel to yourself, as a sort of spiritual discipline, in the same way we engage with prayer or Bible reading. Indeed, prayer and Bible study can be means through which we preach the gospel to ourselves.

Similarly, we see the idea of preaching the gospel to yourself in the approach of the reformer Martin Luther:

> The highest of all God's commands is this, that we ever hold up before our eyes the image of his dear Son, our Lord Jesus Christ. He must daily be to our hearts the perfect mirror, in which we behold how much God loves us and how well, in his infinite goodness, as a faithful God, he has grandly cared for us in that he gave his dear Son for us.[5]

There are many mirrors we could gaze into, but none are as powerful as the mirror of Jesus. As we gaze into our phones, we often see through mirrors of comparison and consumerism; mirrors that distort healthy body image; mirrors that makes us feel *less than*. We see our flaws and failures and compare them with other people's best filtered presentations of themselves.

Instead, we can hold up the mirror of Jesus. *Look*. It is a stimulus. When we look into the mirror of the gospel, and when we confess the truth of God's Word, we see ourselves as loved and accepted. We will surely reflex in the most remarkable ways.

The Effort of Grace

It is only by grace that we can receive the stimulus of the gospel. Colossians 2:6 tells us, 'just as you received Christ Jesus as Lord, continue to live your lives in him'. How did we receive Jesus as Lord? By grace, through faith.[6] We entered the Christian life by grace, through faith, and we continue to live and grow in the Christian faith by grace, through faith. Our 'work', as Jesus said, is to believe.[7] If we go back to the original medical metaphor of a reflex, it is almost like grace opens up the door into the doctor's surgery and gets us in front of the doctor, ready for the stimulus input. Grace grants us access. It positions us for the stimulus.

In recent years there has been a lot of talk about *hyper-grace*. People argue that the concept of grace can be so exaggerated that it becomes error; that it is used as an excuse to live in unholy ways. Perhaps. But I am all about grace. I want as much of it as possible in my life. I want it to abound in me. I want to feed on the gospel of grace daily.

Yet I do think there are some errors that we can slip into when it comes to grace.

One of the phrases I've found myself using again and again when I talk about grace is, 'The effort of grace is surrender.' Yes, grace is fundamentally a free gift. It is something that is received. It can't be earned, and it is not deserved. But I've found that to apply the transformational input of grace into our lives requires intentional effort.

Inputting the transformational gospel of grace does not just happen to us. Nothing in the Christian life just happens to us, as that would negate our free will. God does not 'do it to us'. If it just happened, then there would be huge numbers of passive Christians who become radically transformed into Christ's likeness through their passivity. Rather, as Jerry Bridges writes, 'God's work does not make our effort unnecessary, but rather makes it effective.'[8]

Neither do we strive for grace or earn grace. Instead, as with so many things in the Christian life, we yield to it. We surrender to it. *The effort of grace is surrender.*

I found the late Dallas Willard speaks powerfully into this. He rightly points out that, 'Grace is not opposed to effort, it is opposed to earning. Earning is an attitude. Effort is an action.'[9] He also says, 'In fact, nothing inspires and enhances effort like the experience of grace.'[10] And there is indeed an effort to reflexing with holy living, as it says in Hebrews 12:14, 'Make every effort to live in peace with everyone and to be holy; without holiness no one will see the Lord.'

So, when I refer to the word *reflex*, the last thing I want to do is to give the impression that the Christian life is effortless. It is not. It is light and easy, it is natural, but it requires effort. And that effort is all about inputting the right kinds of stimuli into our lives. The gospel stimulus requires effort in order for it to become a life-shaping habit.

Gospel Amnesia

Perhaps our problem is that we experience what the author Luma Simms calls *gospel amnesia*.[11] We forget the gospel. We forget how good it is. We forget how it changed everything. We forget that it is the source of our peace. We forget how it empowers us to forgive and live in healthy relationship with others. We forget who we were and where we were once heading. We forget who we now are, and who we will be, and our new eternal destination.

The solution is to daily remind ourselves of the gospel. Input the gospel – find ways to make the gospel the greatest stimulus in your life – and you will reflex automatically with a life ever-increasingly more like Jesus.

So, what might it look like to preach the gospel to yourself or to look into the mirror of the gospel? Well, to some extent, I'm going to illustrate various ways in which we might do that in parts two and three of this book. As we find ways to be filled with the love of God, we naturally reflex with love for others; as we build rhythms in our lives of gratitude, we more naturally reflex with generosity, to give just two examples. But it might be helpful to share now something of how we might do that.

When we think of spiritual disciplines, we think of things like reading Scripture, or prayer, worship, communion, and fellowship with other believers. Or we might think of a morning quiet time. And in one sense, that is sort of what I mean by *gospel inputs*. But to be honest, I find the phrase *spiritual disciplines* unhelpful. It makes these things seem a bit like rules – transactional, religious practice. And all of these things can easily tip into religious duty. So, I don't like the term *spiritual disciplines*. Rather, I heard someone once refer to them as *relational rhythms*. I like that.

To the onlooker, the difference between a spiritual discipline and a relational rhythm may be almost indistinguishable, but believe me when I say it makes all the difference. As I write, I have just taken a break to go for a run with a neighbour who is ex-military. As we ran, he reflected on how, for many years, he had to run because he was told to run by someone of a higher rank. If he wanted to progress up the ranks, he needed to do as he was told. But now as we ran, he ran with a different motivation: to strengthen relationship, and for the joy, health and life that flowed out of it. Likewise, I used to have a spiritual discipline of prayer. I did it because God told me to, because the pastor preached that I should. Whereas nowadays I pray more than I have ever prayed – deliberately and intentionally. I set aside time in my diary each day, and for an extended time each month. Why? Because it is life and joy to me, and because I have experienced how it deepens my relationship with Jesus.

Gospel inputs are the things that deepen our relationship with Jesus. It is a bit like when I buy my wife flowers each week or make her a coffee each morning or tell her how lovely she looks each day or take her out for a meal. I don't do these things because it is my marital duty to do them or in order to be a good husband. I do them because I love her. I do them because I'm grateful to have her as my wife. It is my joy and delight to do those things. As I intentionally develop a rhythm of doing these things, rather than doing them as one-offs, they deepen intimacy and relationship. Now, I don't want my relationship with my wife to only be expressed in these structured, or you could say *organised*, times. That's not exactly romantic! I'm fairly convinced that loving relationships require some spontaneity. But when you put in rhythms that express the significance of your relationship and love for one another, you create a culture that means the spontaneous expressions of love flow out naturally. Love drives the structure and organisation of these rhythms, which creates the environment for spontaneous and organic expressions of love to regularly occur.

And so it is with God. When I get up each morning, it is a delight to be able to open the Bible and start to read. As I do so, I hear his whisper to my soul. I see his unchanging and satisfying character in every verse, on every page. I'm reminded not so much of what I need to do, but of that which has been done for me that I could have never done for myself. I am *gospelling* myself. I am not doing a daily Bible reading plan because I *have* to, but rather because in doing so I grow in intimacy with Jesus.

I then start to play some worship music. Songs that remind me of who Jesus is and what he has done for me. I sing out the truth of the cross and the empty grave. As I do so, I am proclaiming the gospel to myself.

I start to pray and to thank God for who he is – seeking his face, not his hand. I start to remind myself of his very great and precious promises. I'm not praying about what I want God to do for me. I am proclaiming what has already been done for me. I am inputting the gospel into my life. Sure, at some point towards the end of this time, I will bring my prayer requests before the Lord. I will petition him. But by the time I do this, I'm doing it from a point of faith, presence and intimacy. I ask of him with gospel confidence.

When I input the gospel like this, in a regular relational rhythm, I then find that I am more likely to connect with God at other, unplanned times. When I am out walking the dog, I find I spontaneously turn my attention to God with thanksgiving and gratitude. I thank God for the wonderful city in which

I live. I thank him for the many family members and friends we have in the city. I thank him for my health. I thank him that I can know him and enjoy him. It is a choice, like anything in life. I can choose to listen to a comedy podcast. I can choose to think about the things that are annoying me or the people who have upset me – or I can get lost in the wonder of who Jesus is.

Gospelling Together

This idea of *gospelling* isn't just for us as individuals. It's something we can do with others. At the church I lead, we share communion as a staff body every morning. We remind ourselves and each other of what Christ has already done for us. When I introduced this idea, the push back was that it would mean staff would get less work done. Absolutely! Exactly! As we work less and abide more, we bear more fruit. As we input the stimulus of the gospel into our lives, we reflex in a way that transforms the world around us, in a way that brings good news to the people we rub shoulders with. Hungry people get fed. Lonely people get included. Addicted people find freedom. Fearful people find peace.

My observation is that this is how it always works. When we build rhythms into our lives of connection with other Christians to remind ourselves and each other of the gospel, we reflex in ways that bring good news to the world around us. In our church, we encourage people to be part of community groups, groups that focus on seeking Jesus together, inputting the gospel in their lives and letting the Holy Spirit lead them in sharing the good news with people around them. It is not a surprise to me that I am always hearing stories from our church community groups of how people took flowers around to a lonely neighbour, or how they all chipped in to buy a struggling family a washing machine, or that they took the kids of a family experiencing stress and pressure out for a day of fun. Communities of believers who input the gospel together reflex with good news to the world around them. Honestly, I am not sure we get the same sort of natural outcomes when we make small groups about 'me and my needs'.

Let me give you another example of a communal gospelling: fasting. I don't know what you think of when you think of fasting, but it seems to me that there are two ways we can view it: either as religious duty for the spiritual elite, or through the lens of the gospel. For many years, I viewed it as the former, and let me tell you it was not very appealing. Once a year, I would try to do a five-day fast along with my church, as a way of petitioning God for breakthrough at the start of a new year. Boy, was it hard work! It was joyless. I could not work out why God would want me to be so miserable. But because there were things I needed God to do for me, for others, for the city, I engaged with it. Fasting was my religious duty.

A number of years ago, someone shared with me a radically different way of viewing fasting, taken from Matthew 9:14–15:

> Then John's disciples came and asked him, 'How is it that we and the Pharisees fast often, but your disciples do not fast?' Jesus answered, 'How can the guests of the bridegroom mourn while he is with them? The time will come when the bridegroom will be taken from them; then they will fast.'

I realised I had been fasting like a Pharisee. But in these verses, we see that fasting is about *intimacy*. If you have not heard that before, pause and make sure you have got it. Fasting is about intimacy. Jesus is saying that while he, the Bridegroom, was present with his disciples there was no need to fast. But a time was coming when the Bridegroom would be separated from the bride, and *then* they will fast. Fasting is about turning the longing for food into a longing for Jesus. It's about longing for his presence here and now, as heaven invades earth, but it is also longing, in that ultimate sense, for when the Bridegroom will return for his bride, the church, and we will be united forever at the marriage supper of the lamb. Oh, how I long for that day! It is a longing that has intensified through fasting. At my church we call this type of fasting the *Bridegroom Fast*. Practically, I don't think it matters too much *how* you do it; it is more about *why* you do it. But, as an example, we invite everyone to eat their evening meal on the Monday evening, then fast twenty-four hours, breaking their fast with their evening meal on the Tuesday evening. It is a weekly, communal, relational rhythm. I can't evidence this, but I believe it is one of the most powerful things we have done as a church. Certainly, it has been transformational in my own life. Fasting has become a joy. It has become a way of gospelling myself. As I fast, I am asking Jesus for more of his presence in my life. That is the input, the stimulus.

I am not saying for one moment that you should do the things I do; in the way I do them. This is simply to illustrate what daily preaching the gospel to myself looks like *for me*. Whatever way you do it, the question is this: is it a relational rhythm of intimacy and abiding, or is it religious duty and striving? You see, you can have two people who by all intents and purposes live the same way. Both pray and read their Bibles. Both go to church, serve and tithe. The thing is, for one it is religious duty and leads to weariness, whereas for the other it is life-giving, energising and joyful. If you have been a Christian for any length of time, you will probably know exactly what I am talking about because it's likely you've had seasons of both: seasons when it was wearying and lifeless, and seasons when it was pure joy. What is the difference? It is the difference between religion and relationship. One of those two people has gospel amnesia, a distant memory of the gospel; the other, a mind and heart being constantly filled with the good news.

The gospel is to be proclaimed to oneself and to the world. And when we do so, it is transformative. It requires a sacrifice of time. It requires intentionality, effort and prioritisation. But don't let it lead you onto the slippery slope of religion. For the Christian, religion is a form of gospel amnesia. It relegates the good news of life with Jesus into a singular, distant, past event: the moment of conversion. But when we preach the gospel to ourselves daily, we are reminded each day that the good news is about a relationship. Relationships change us. They shape who we are. And relationship with Jesus completely transforms our lives, every single day.

This is how Fred Sanders puts it in his book *The Deep Things of God*:

A gospel which is only about the moment of conversion but does not extend to every moment of life in Christ is too small. A gospel that gets your sins forgiven but offers no power for transformation is too small. A gospel that must be measured by your own moral conduct, social conscience, or religious experience is too small. A gospel that rearranges the components of your life but does not put you personally in the presence of God is too small.[12]

Is your gospel too small? Is it a distant memory? Is it just religious transactions? Allow your gospel to grow. To get bigger. Start to build relational rhythms of preaching the gospel to your soul, and you will reflex in the most transformative ways.

QUESTIONS FOR DISCUSSION

1. Do you continue to preach the gospel to yourself, or is it just something you did when you first came to faith?

2. How big is your gospel? Has your gospel become too small? Are there areas or aspects of your life that the gospel doesn't seem to have touched or impacted?

3. What do your relational rhythms look like? Are they about relational intimacy or are they religious duty and striving?

3

THE COVENANT-KINGDOM REFLEX

As we input the truth of our covenant identity,
we reflex with kingdom activity.

All of us have read life-changing books ... books that resonated so deeply with us that we begin to interpret life through
the concepts and ideas we discovered in the pages. Mike
Breen's book *Covenant and Kingdom* is one such book for me.[1]
If you haven't already, I wholeheartedly recommend you read
it. I want to try to summarise some of its key ideas here, and
then use them as a springboard into my first reflex example,
what I call *the covenant-kingdom reflex*.

Simply put, there are two main themes that run throughout
Scripture: *covenant* and *kingdom*. Like the two horizontal and
vertical directions of thread that run through a piece of fabric
(the warp and weft), these two themes weave their way from
Genesis to Revelation. They are also like the two lenses of a

pair of glasses, through which we can read Scripture; a bit like a
hermeneutic. Covenant and kingdom are also like two legs that
power a push bike. Both legs are equally important. One may
be dominant, but it is in the rhythm between the two that we
find flow and momentum. It is in the rhythm that we find ease.
In essence:

> Covenant is about identity. Relationship. Who we are.
> Kingdom is about activity. Responsibility. What we do.

Covenant can be considered as the terms and conditions of
a relationship. When God entered into relationship with
Abraham (then called Abram), he set out the terms and conditions of the relationship through the corridor of blood. The
covenant was 'cut'. Indeed, the ancient origins of the word covenant, in Hebrew *brit* means *to cut*. You can read about it in
Genesis chapters 12–17. The essence of this covenant can be
found in Genesis 12:1–3,

> The LORD had said to Abram, 'Go from your country,
> your people and your father's household to the land I
> will show you. I will make you into a great nation, and
> I will bless you; I will make your name great, and you
> will be a blessing. I will bless those who bless you, and
> whoever curses you I will curse; and all peoples on
> earth will be blessed through you.'

Through the covenant, Abram's name was changed to
Abraham, a change of identity. The covenant speaks of what
God will do for Abram: 'I will … I will …' It's about relational
commitment.

Today we might think of marriage as an example of a covenant. When I married my wife, my identity changed. I went from being John, a single guy who pretty much did what he wanted when he wanted, to John, the husband of Kirsten. I made solemn promises to love, honour and cherish Kirsten. For Kirsten, this covenant involved a change of name; she took on the Harding family name. That is covenant.

A similar thing happened in my early twenties when I found a place of belonging in a church community called Frontline Church, the church I would later go on to lead. As I threw in my lot, I began to increasingly commit my time and money into this fledgling community, as an expression of my commitment to God. In time, I found I became a 'Frontliner'. This Christian community of believers profoundly influenced my sense of identity, as I gradually grew in relational connection with those around me. That is covenant.

Through the work of Christ on the cross, we have entered into a new covenant relationship with God. The covenant of blood was cut on the cross, and as we passed through it, we went from death to life. This is what God has done for us. We take on a new name, a new family identity. We become sons and daughters of a new family. Covenant is at the heart of the gospel.

If covenant speaks of identity and relationship, kingdom speaks of activity and responsibility. When we think of kingdom in the natural realm, we might think of kings and castles; of something that is advancing; of territory. In the same way, the lens of kingdom is about God's people living under the kingship of Jesus, extending and advancing the values of his kingdom throughout the world.

Jesus told many kingdom parables.[2] These stories help us understand that the kingdom of God breaks into the kingdom of this world as the gospel is advanced. It is like seed that grows and multiplies. It is like yeast that raises the dough. Whenever we live out the values of the kingdom of heaven, whenever we bring the justice or peace or healing of heaven into a situation on earth, there the kingdom is being advanced and established.

Feeding the hungry is kingdom activity.

Setting the oppressed free is kingdom activity.

Binding up the broken-hearted is kingdom activity.

Housing the homeless is kingdom activity.

Proclaiming the gospel is kingdom activity.

In doing all these things, we are bringing the kingdom of heaven to earth.

The two great themes of covenant and kingdom run through the entire Bible, and they help us understand *how* to live the Christian life.

In his book, Mike Breen powerfully makes the point that although both covenant and kingdom are equal, we have to engage with covenant first. Relationship first. Identity first. All of our kingdom activity has to flow out of our covenant identity. You could say it's a reflex.

Transformed People Transform People

In Genesis 1:27–28, we see that humans are first made in the image of God. That is our identity. *Then*, they are commanded to be fruitful and fill the earth. To rule and steward. That is activity. Identity followed by activity. Covenant then kingdom.

In Genesis 12, as humans begin to spread out and populate the earth, God speaks to a Bronze-Age nomad called Abram, plucked out of obscurity. Remember, this is before God has established a chosen people group (the Israelites) or a chosen land (Israel). Abram encounters God, the covenant is established, and then Abram is sent on a journey to the Promised Land, into kingdom activity.

Fast-forward some five hundred years, and we read in Exodus 1–3 how Moses also has this experience of the covenant-kingdom reflex. Moses has somewhat of an identity crisis when he first encounters God, the *I AM*, at the burning bush. Born a slave, raised a prince, and now hiding as a fugitive, Moses seems an unlikely character to come into covenant with God. But it is from this encounter that he receives his acceptance and identity and is then sent out to liberate the people from Egypt.

After the liberation of the Israelites from Egypt, God's people are trying to figure out how to live in the desert and how to follow God's ways. When Aaron the high priest first proclaims the words of *the blessing* over the people, it seems to be without effect. Mere words. But when he spends time in the tent of meeting, in the presence of God, and *then* speaks out those same words, his proclamation impacts the people. God's glory falls on the people, they shout for joy and fall on their faces in worship.[3]

David also displays this reflex brilliantly as he cultivates intimacy and a heart of worship as a shepherd before God calls him and appoints him king.[4]

And again, with the prophet Isaiah, he first saw the Lord in his holy place.[5] One of the angelic beings took a live coal from the altar and touched Isaiah's mouth with it, cleansing him of his sin. And Isaiah's response to this encounter was to say, 'Here am I. Send me!' (Isaiah 6:8). Covenant identity reflexing with kingdom activity.

Not surprisingly, we see the same pattern in the ministry of Jesus. At his baptism, Jesus' identity is affirmed. His relationship with the Father is revealed, as the Father speaks over him, 'This is my Son, whom I love; with him I am well pleased' (Matthew 17:5). It is a statement of covenant. At that point in his life, Jesus had not performed any miracles. He had not preached any sermons. He had not cast out any demons or called any disciples. In many ways, Jesus had done nothing. And yet the Father was pleased with the Son. Before any kingdom activity, Jesus' covenant identity was affirmed. And from there, Jesus was compelled into the desert and into ministry.

When Jesus appointed his twelve apostles, he modelled this covenant-kingdom pattern to them. In Mark 3:14, 'He appointed twelve that they might be with him and that he might send them out to preach.' They were called first to be with him in relationship, and then to go out and preach.

Kingdom activity is as natural as blinking, a reflex ... *if* you have the right stimulus. Input *covenant*, and you will reflex with *kingdom*. Spend time experiencing the Father's words of affirmation, hear the Father saying, 'Well done, son' or 'I love you, daughter', and you will reflex by making a difference in the world around you. That is why I find myself saying all the time to the church I lead:

Transformed people transform people.

Transformed people can't do anything *but* transform the world around them. As we grow in our covenant identity, really understanding and believing who we are in Christ, we start to naturally live differently. We start to operate in a new level of kingdom authority because we have grown in our royal identity. This was the experience of the earliest church in Acts. As they devoted themselves to the Word, to worship, to fellowship, to the gospel input of breaking bread, as they served one another in covenant community, the kingdom reflex was extraordinary; God himself grew their number.[6]

And we see this in Paul's unpacking of salvation by grace, through faith, in Ephesians 2:8–10:

> For it is by grace you have been saved, through faith
> – and this is not from yourselves, it is the gift of God
> – not by works, so that no one can boast. For we are
> God's handiwork, created in Christ Jesus to do good
> works, which God prepared in advance for us to do.

When you have seen the reflex principle, it's easy to recognise it in verses like these. Receive the gift (input); reflex with good works (outcome).

Similarly, in Colossians 1, God *fills us* 'with the knowledge of his will through all the wisdom and understanding that the Spirit gives' (verse 9) in order that we may 'live a life worthy of the Lord and please him in every way: bearing fruit in every good work' (verse 10). This is the language of reflex: God fills us; we bear fruit.

And in 1 Thessalonians 1:3, 'We remember before our God and Father your work produced by faith, your labour prompted by love, and your endurance inspired by hope in our Lord Jesus Christ.' This is such a good verse for understanding the covenant-kingdom reflex. Work reflexing out of faith. Labour reflexing out of love. Endurance reflexing out of hope in Christ. The inputs of faith, hope and love.

As I have inputted the gospel and my identity in Christ, I have found it has radically changed the way I pray. I pray as a son of God, rather than as a servant of God. It has increased the levels of breakthrough I experience through prayer. It has changed how I engage with the world around me. I find I am not striving for the approval of others because I know how much I am loved. I can play my part in seeing God's kingdom come on earth, without being distracted by how other people may or may not receive me. When you understand who you are, you pray for the kingdom to come and heaven to invade earth. When you understand who you are, you work to advance the kingdom of heaven. It is just what you do. It is the family business.

I recently heard the story of a young couple in our church community who are worship leaders. During one of the UK's Covid-19 lockdowns of 2020, when church buildings were closed, they began to express their worship through kingdom activity. They began to tidy up the alleyway that runs along the back of their house. They pulled up the weeds and cleared out the extensive rubbish that had accumulated. Their neighbours began to notice, and even joined in the clear-up. They repaired broken walls, painted garden gates, and potted plants. Residents bought garden furniture, tables and chairs, and put them into this shared alleyway space to form a communal area. Towards the end of the project, they set up an outdoor cinema screen. Neighbours who had been fearfully trapped and hiding in their homes met one another, learnt one another's names and built relationship. Their endeavours even made it into the local and national press! The thing was, for this worship-leading couple, it was such a natural thing for them to do. One couple, impacted by the presence of God, transformed the community around them. Making a difference in the world around us is the natural reflex response to a life of worship.[7]

Right identity reflexes with right authority. We have been clothed with Christ. We have been robed with righteousness. We have been commissioned with Christ's authority. We are ambassadors of the Most High King. When you know that, when you really believe that, then you know that when you speak, you are speaking as if it is the very words of God.[8] For out of the *overflow* of the heart (place of belief) the mouth speaks.[9] You can speak and release the peace and justice and provision of heaven into the world around you. You can speak out and halt the advancement of the kingdom of darkness – because when the devil sees you, he sees you for who you really are. He sees you clothed with Christ. Hidden in Christ.

Right identity reflexes with right activity. Authority reflexing with power. This is the covenant-kingdom reflex.

Vital Signs of Life

A reflex can also act as a diagnostic tool. In the medical world, if there is no blink, no swing of the knee, we know something is wrong. The same is true in the spiritual realm. If we were to take a cold, hard look at our lives, what evidence of kingdom impact would we find? If we were to review our diaries or monitor our social media screen use, what would that say about how we use our time and how we prioritise the advancement of the kingdom? What about if we were to review our bank account and spending habits? How is the kingdom of darkness being pushed back and the kingdom of heaven released through the way we live? It is a challenging thought indeed, one well worth taking a moment to reflect, journal and discuss with other believers.

If we examine our lives for the reflex action of kingdom impact and find the reflex is dull or even dead, let me tell you what the solution is. Or rather what the solution is not. The solution is not to do more. It is not to get all guilty, or even psyched-up for action. The remedy is not to go out and give to the poor, feed the hungry, care for the orphan and widow (as important as all those things are). And that is certainly not the ask of this book. The remedy is to input the gospel. The remedy is the stimulus of covenant identity. To input into our lives the truth of who God is and who we are in him. To deepen in our love for God. To allow the Holy Spirit access to our hearts so that we can be transformed into who God calls us to be. To build community with those who can help us, especially when the brokenness of life and past experiences make it difficult to input that stimuli into ourselves. And to do so with confident expectation that as we do this, we will begin to reflex with kingdom impact.

I mean, think about it. The first and greatest command is simply this, 'Love the Lord your God with all your heart and with all your soul and with all your mind and with all your strength'; and the second greatest command is: 'Love your neighbour as yourself' (Mark 12:30–31).

How much should we love God? Jesus says with *all*. All of us. Every fibre and ounce of our being. But how can we love our neighbour if we have given all our love to God? What love would we have left for others if all 100 per cent has gone to God? Can you see the reflex? I would suggest that loving our neighbour is a *reflex* to loving God and loving ourselves. As we deepen in covenant – expressed as love for God and love for ourselves as made in the image of God – we find that we are filled to overflowing with love for others. We reflex.

A Covenant-Kingdom Structure

As we now start to unpack in more detail how this reflex plays out in our lives, I believe that this dual covenant-kingdom lens will help us journey more easily through this book. As such, I have separated out the rest of the book into two parts: *covenant reflexes* – outcomes and responses to the gospel that develop identity and relationships, and deepen intimacy; and *kingdom reflexes* – outcomes and responses that impact the world around us and advance the kingdom of God. In both cases, the stimulus is the same – the gospel. Input the gospel, and you will reflex with both *internal* transformation (covenant, for example in holiness, love, joy and generosity) and *external* transformation (kingdom, such as victory, leadership and sharing the good news).

Input the gospel, and you will begin to see God's glorious, transformative reflex at work in your life – the power of the gospel to change everything.

QUESTIONS FOR DISCUSSION

1. Can you think of other examples where you can see the covenant-kingdom reflex principle at work (either in your own life, a Bible character or the life of someone you know)?

2. What is the significance of 'covenant, before kingdom' as we move away from an 'outcomes-focused' way of following Jesus?

3. To what extent do you see yourself as an ambassador of the Most High King? How can you grow in your royal identity?

PART 2

COVENANT REFLEXES

4

THE HOLINESS
REFLEX

As we gaze at our glorious God, we reflex with holiness.

As a young Christian, I spent a lot of time and effort trying
to be holy so that God could use me. Boy, was it exhausting!
The problem with *trying* to be holy, aside from the fact that it's
not biblical, is that when you 'fail', you experience shame and
guilt, and when you 'succeed', you experience pride and self-
righteousness.[1] I don't want to sound judgemental about the
sermons I sat under, but what I heard was never-ending to-do
lists and 'useful tips' on how to live a holy life.

The church majored on good advice to achieve holiness.
The gospel, on the contrary, reminds us that *in Christ*, we are
holy.

To be holy, in the most basic sense, means to be pure and
clean enough to be set apart for special use. And the topic of
holiness has become somewhat controversial among followers

of Jesus today. If you have never engaged in this heated debate, good for you, keep it that way! It seems to polarise people into one of two sides. There are those on one side who say it is all about grace. You have to do nothing. Their opponents rightly point out that there are loads of New Testament verses that instruct believers to live holy lives. On the other side, there are those who emphasise that there are things you need to do in order to be holy or become more holy. Their opponents rightly point out that not only is salvation a work of grace and the Holy Spirit, but so is sanctification – the process of being made holy.

You might be pleased to know that I don't think this is a helpful debate to get into here. But I do want to offer some thoughts on how holiness is a reflex to the gospel at work in our lives.

As we think about our covenant reflexes, it is important to remind ourselves of the distinction between the Old Testament covenant and the New Testament covenant. This is why Jesus' invitation to come under his light and easy tallit-yoke was so revolutionary. Before Jesus, the old covenant essentially said, '*If* I do x, y, z *then* I will be blessed or saved or holy.' As I've already mentioned, this is religion. I know from my own life, and having spent time talking to many people, that we can so easily tip into this. We end up in self-effort or self-righteousness. Many of us read the Bible in this way, viewing it as a massive list of rules; the nice things we should do, and the naughty things we shouldn't. But the Bible is first and foremost about God, who he is, and what he has done, is doing and will do. It is not primarily about us and what we should do. So, if reading the Bible, listening to sermons, or trying to live the Christian life leaves you feeling weary and under a heavy burden, then maybe you too have been reading the Bible incorrectly. Maybe you have got caught up in self-effort. If that describes you, then this chapter is for you! I pray that it will help you live under the light and easy yoke of Jesus. I pray that as you preach the gospel to yourself more and more, you will find that you naturally reflex with a deep desire to live in a way that pleases him.

The Holiness Paradox

One key question we might ask is, *Am I holy?* Or, *To what extent am I holy?* As I read the Scriptures, it seems there are two true and yet apparently contradictory answers to these questions. In other words, the answer is paradoxical. This ought not to surprise us. Embracing paradox is essential to understanding Scripture. Mystery is woven throughout the Christian faith. We believe in a God who is both one and three. Paradox. We believe in a Saviour who lived on earth as both God and man. Fully God, fully man, yet one. Paradox. As followers of Jesus, we are simultaneously satisfied and long for more. Paradox. We should not test God,[2] and yet we should test God *in this*.[3] Paradox.

And so it is with holiness. If you are a follower of Jesus, you are holy. Colossians 3:12 says you are part of 'God's chosen people, holy and dearly loved'. But how holy? That is an interesting question. Religion seeks to grade holiness, but that's not how it works with God. You are either holy or you are not. So how holy are you? You are holy enough for the Holy Spirit to live within you. You are holy enough to be called a saint, for that is who you are.[4]

In 1 Corinthians 6:11, Paul uses the past tense to emphasise the truth that we have been made holy: 'But you *were* washed, you *were* sanctified, you *were* justified in the name of the Lord' (italics mine). Remember *sanctified* means *to be made holy.* Likewise, in Hebrews 10:10 we read that 'we *have been* made holy through the sacrifice of the body of Jesus Christ once for all' (italics mine). In Acts 26:18, the gospel Paul preaches to the Gentiles is an invitation for their sins to be forgiven and to receive a place 'among those who *are* sanctified by faith in [God]' (italics mine).

And yet the Bible also teaches that we are *to be* holy. We are to 'purify ourselves from everything that contaminates body and spirit, perfecting holiness out of reverence for God' (2 Corinthians 7:1). So not only does the Bible use the past tense for holiness, but also the present and future tense. Hebrews 10:14 says, 'For by one sacrifice he has made perfect forever those who are being made holy.' That is a great verse for capturing this paradox. Jesus *made perfect* those who are *being made* holy.

We are holy. We are being made holy. Both are true.

So how do we make sense of this paradox? Well one helpful way of embracing both truths is to understand the difference between our *status* and our *state.* I am not sure where this distinction comes from; I picked it up many years ago while at theological college. It is not perfect language, but it has nonetheless helped me and many others to enjoy both the holiness we've been given *and* grow in our holiness.

By *status,* I mean how God sees you. This is, of course, the greatest reality. God sees you as holy. Ephesians 1:4 says, 'For he chose us in him before the creation of the world to be holy and blameless *in his sight*' (italics mine). He sees you as holy. Why? Because you have been clothed with the righteousness of his Son, you are *in* Christ.[5] So your status, your identity and title over your life is *holy.*

By *state* I mean how you live day by day. I don't know about you, but I still do some unholy things. There are holy things I should do that I don't do. And there are unholy thoughts, words and deeds that are evident in my life each day. That is my *state*. You might be inclined to think that this is the real you, but actually *how God sees you* is a far more accurate picture of who you really are than how you see yourself.

The challenge is to bring our *state* in line with our *status*. How do we do that? We input the right stimulus so that holy living is the natural reflex outcome; the way we live, our state, is transformed.

Holiness Imparted Through God's Glory

The holiness reflex helps us to understand the true nature of what it means for us to be holy, not as a certificate awarded to us for merit or good behaviour, but rather the process of how a holy God shares with us his holy nature. And the way God shares his holy nature with us is through his glory.

Glory is a big concept. In fact, it is somewhat of a theological summary word, a biblical catch-all. It is different from other words we might use to describe the essence or attributes of God. Put simply, glory is the revelation of God's essence or attributes. When we experience glory, we encounter something of God. So, for example, we know that God is love. Love is both an attribute of God and the very essence of God. But when we experience that and it becomes tangible to us, that is a moment of glory: love revealed.

Now, in this chapter we are thinking about holiness. If we play the concept of holiness through our definition of glory, then glory describes an encounter with the holiness of God.

To help us understand this, let's consider for a moment the life of Moses.

Moses, the leader of God's people, was commanded by God to go up Mount Sinai to receive the Ten Commandments. On that mountain, Moses decided he was going to make a request of God. He said to God, 'show me your glory' (Exodus 33:18). In other words, Moses was asking God to reveal his nature to him. So God responded to his request. He hid Moses into a tiny crack in the mountainside and passed by, allowing Moses to see his back, and as he did so, God revealed his glory by proclaiming his nature and character.

> Then the LORD came down in the cloud and stood there with him and proclaimed his name, the LORD. And he passed in front of Moses, proclaiming, 'The LORD, the LORD, the compassionate and gracious God, slow to anger, abounding in love and faithfulness, maintaining love to thousands, and forgiving wickedness, rebellion and sin. Yet he does not leave the guilty unpunished; he punishes the children and their children for the sin of the parents to the third and fourth generation.'
>
> Exodus 34:5-7

Moses asked to see God's glory, and God passed in front of Moses, as God proclaimed his nature. A moment of glory. The glory of God is the revealed nature of God. It is his character, his essence, made manifest, tangible, felt. Glory is the physical revelation of who God is. A God who is compassionate and gracious. A God who is slow to anger and abounding in love and faithfulness. Glory is more than just knowing truth; it is *experiencing* it. John Piper describes it this way:

The glory of God is the manifest beauty of his holiness. It is the going-public of his holiness. It is the way he puts his holiness on display for people to apprehend. So, the glory of God is the holiness of God made manifest.[6]

The Hebrew word for glory is *kavod*, and it speaks of *weightiness*. Experiencing the glory of God is different to knowing about who God is; it is feeling the weight of who God is resting upon you. It is basking in the warmth of his radiance in such a way that causes us to radiate with his light and warmth. It's a stimulus, a holy God allowing us to experience and enjoy his holiness.

Whenever Moses encountered the presence of God, or the glory of God, Moses would have to cover his face with a veil.[7] The experience of spending time in the radiant light and majesty of God was so immense that it caused Moses' face to shine, and that radiance was simply too much for the people – they were afraid to come near him. But as time passed, the bright shining radiance upon Moses' face would fade until, once again, he entered into the presence of the Lord, in the holy place of the tabernacle tent.

In 2 Corinthians 3:14–18, our new covenant experience is compared with that of Moses. In verse 18, it says, 'And we all, who with unveiled faces contemplate the Lord's glory, are being transformed into his image with ever-increasing glory, which comes from the Lord, who is the Spirit.' Something incredible is happening in this verse. It says that as we gaze at Jesus, we are transformed from glory to glory, in ever-increasing measures. Wow! Like Moses, we too radiate with the glory of God. Not with veiled faces, but with *unveiled* faces. Not in a way that fades and diminishes, but in a way that increases, with ever-increasing measures of glory. As we experience glory, we reflex with glory.

Encountering Christ, as we gaze at him and experience his glory, is the input, the stimulus. As we encounter him, we become glorified. In other words, we reflex by taking on his nature. We reflex with more compassion and grace towards others. We become slower to anger. We abound more in love and faithfulness. We become holy as he is holy.[8] These aspects of God's nature are seen and experienced by those around us, because glory is his nature revealed.

How can this happen? Well, grace gives access, opening the door to encounter and giving us permission to 'enter in' and experience a holy God in whose presence we are transformed. The picture I used before was of grace being the access to the doctor's surgery, where we can then receive the stimulus for the reflex.

In the ancient Eastern Orthodox traditions, they have a theological term called *theosis*. Essentially, it means union with God resulting in absorbing the nature of God. It is outrageous, almost blasphemous. We almost dare not say it. What sort of a God would elevate fallen and broken humanity to a point of sharing his same nature? But that is exactly what the Scriptures teach us. As we gaze at Jesus, we are being transformed into his likeness. Holiness is a reflex to looking at Jesus.[9]

Behold-Believe-Behave

So, what is the process that is happening when we experience God's glory? How are we transformed into his likeness?

Well, I would argue that *what we gaze upon, we become like.* ... If you didn't catch that, just read it again and let it sink

in: *what we gaze upon, we become like.* That is how God designed it to be. It's a reflex. After all, this whole story starts with
you and me being made in the image of God.[10] We are made
to be mirrors. We are made to reflect the God of glory, and we
reflect his nature as we behold him.

I call this the *behold-believe-behave reflex.* If you want to
behave right, you have to believe right. If you want to believe
right, you have to behold right. What you gaze upon, you become like. So, for example, if I want to step out in faith and
take a risk (*behaviour*), then I have to believe that God has got
me. He holds me, and I am safe in his hands (*belief*). But if I
am going to believe that, I have to *behold* right. I have to see
him on every page of Scripture as a God who is utterly faithful,
utterly reliable, and who will never leave me or abandon me,
for that is who he is.

Jesus said, 'The eye is the lamp of the body. If your eyes
are healthy, your whole body will be full of light' (Matthew
6:22). It is a reflex. It starts with seeing something of God, a
glory moment. Behold God, and you have the right input,
the right stimulus. You will reflex with glorious light and
transformation. Get it wrong, behold wrongly, and unholy
behaviour happens naturally. The Bible says of Lot, for example, that he pitched his tent near Sodom, a city synonymous
with sin.[11] Imagine the scene: every morning Lot wakes up,
gets out of bed, stretches, puts the kettle on and opens the
curtains of his tent. What is the first thing he sees? Sodom,
the city of sin. It's not surprising he soon ended up living
there. Or consider King David, awake at night on the roof of
his palace. He sees a beautiful woman, Bathsheba, bathing.
He has her brought to him, sleeps with her, and she becomes
pregnant. The repercussions of this sinful behaviour were

enormous and echoed throughout the kingdom and into the next generation.[12]

Where we focus our gaze makes all the difference. I think that is why idolatry is such a big issue in the Old Testament,[13] and why it remains such a big issue for believers today. In the ancient Near East, an idol was usually made of wood, stone or precious metal, representing a god. Idol worship, in its most basic sense, was to behold the idol. Seems harmless enough. But what we discover is that certain behaviours always reflexed out of this beholding. The behaviour of the worshipper reflexed the nature of the deity. In other words, the worshipper become like what or who they gazed at. After all, what is worship if it is not *focus*? As the late American poet Mary Oliver wrote, 'Attention is the beginning of devotion.'[14]

Perhaps the clearest example of God condemning idol worship is in the book of Amos. God's people had become no different to any other nation, worshipping the gods of the neighbouring Canaanites.[15] They were worshipping the deities of sex and fertility (Asherah), and weather (Baal), and war (Anat). The problem was, these idols were immoral, and so they required immoral forms of worship. For example, the worship of Asherah, the god of fertility, involved sex with temple prostitutes as an act of worship. In other words, beholding an idol of sex involved partaking in sexual immorality. (I think this speaks strongly into today's culture, with its idolatry of sex and the availability of pornography.) To behold the idol of war, meant partaking in violent behaviour. This manifested in blood-letting and child sacrifice.

What we behold, we become like. This works both for positive and for negative, a healthy or unhealthy gaze.

I remember a 'successful' friend, a Christian who was working in finance in the centre of London, telling me that his biggest challenge was seeing the high-end cars, watches and suits all around him. Not that there is anything wrong with those things in and of themselves. But he found himself increasingly drawn to them, and spent increasingly more of his money on them too. He described it as an identity change, a gradual assimilation, almost like he drifted out of his identity as a follower of Jesus.

David Foster Wallace says,

There is actually no such thing as atheism. There is no such thing as not worshipping. Everybody worships. The only choice we get is what to worship. And the compelling reason for maybe choosing some sort of god or spiritual-type thing to worship—be it JC or Allah, be it YHWH or the Wiccan Mother Goddess, or the Four Noble Truths, or some inviolable set of ethical principles—is that pretty much anything else you worship will eat you alive. If you worship money and things, if they are where you tap real meaning in life, then you will never have enough, never feel you have enough. It's the truth. Worship your body and beauty and sexual allure and you will always feel ugly. And when time and age start showing, you will die a million deaths before they finally grieve you. On one level, we all know this stuff already. It's been codified as myths, proverbs, clichés, epigrams, parables; the skeleton of every great story. The whole trick is keeping the truth up front in daily consciousness.[16]

So we all worship, because we all gaze at something, or someone. And when we gaze at something, we are completely captivated, giving it our undivided, full attention. I think this is what Jesus was reminding Martha of in Luke 10:41–42, that Mary had 'chosen what is better' – sitting at the Lord's feet, gazing … giving her wonderful Saviour her undivided attention.

I am sure we can all think of examples like that in our own lives, where our identity and behaviour have been influenced through what we behold. If you can't think of any personal examples, why not take a look at your online browsing history and ask if it reveals any idols in your life! Hebrews 12:2 calls us to fix our eyes on Jesus. The Bible offers us many ways for us to put our gaze on him. We gaze by reading and absorbing his Word, the truth that reminds us of who he is. We gaze by worshipping, by lifting up our eyes to look upon our glorious and amazing God.

We can learn to gaze by encouraging one another in our Christian communities. Perhaps in these communities and discipleship relationships, we need to talk more about those things that fill our vision. I personally have found it so helpful to be in accountable relationships with other Christian men who have loved me enough to ask me about my gaze, and to challenge me to keep my eyes fixed on Jesus.

We call this simple tool *accountability*, and it is a relational rhythm, or spiritual discipline, that has helped me to learn how to behold well. Accountability for the Christian is not about spiritual policing. Rather, it's about asking an individual or a couple of other people to 'poke' us in the eye, to *be* that stimulus. Those I'm accountable to will ask me if I'm working as a reflex to grace, or if I've fallen back into striving and earning. Small, regular accountability groups are powerful means through which we can gospel ourselves and one another. Small groups with a gospel focus have consistently helped me to fall deeper and deeper in love with Jesus, and in doing so, to reflex with holiness. At their best, they have called me back into intimacy, and therefore holiness (as opposed to calling me into holiness as good behaviour).

Christians often grab hold of the idea that if they can just engage more in spiritual disciplines, they will somehow become more holy. It is an understandable conclusion to come to, given the human inclination towards religion: to work to earn God's approval. Rather, spiritual disciplines, or relational rhythms, are useful only to the extent to which they help us gaze at Jesus, to see him and behold him more clearly.

I have observed this consistently in my own life and in the lives of those around me who radiate Jesus. No longer do we need to read the Bible to learn about ourselves and what we must do for God. Instead we gaze into the Scriptures to behold Jesus, to see his satisfying nature on every page. Our prayer language becomes far more concerned in articulating, to the best of our limited ability, the majesty of who God is, rather than simply rehearsing our spiritual shopping lists. Yes, there are so many wonderful worship songs we can listen to, songs that paint a picture of the challenges of life and how God wants to use us to do the impossible. But they are not the ones that make it into my morning devotional playlists. I find I am drawn to songs that simply captivate me with the beauty of who Jesus is. The power of all these relational rhythms of devotion, especially when walked out in community, is that they help us to give Jesus our full and undivided attention. And this is the essence of holiness: being undivided. It is why we reflex with holiness when we gaze upon God.

As we gaze on God, we become like him. As we root out all of the other idols in our lives, and behold him alone, we reflex with holy living. We are changed from glory to glory.

So, fix your eyes on Jesus. Draw close to him, by grace, and behold him. Encounter him in the beauty of his holiness. And as you do so, you will find that you reflex. Your life will look more and more like his, a mirror reflecting his glory to those around you.

QUESTIONS FOR DISCUSSION

1. How does the difference between our *status* and our *state* help you to understand the reflex of holiness?

2. As you reflect on your average day, what do you typically gaze at? What impact does your beholding have on your behaviour?

3. What might the *effort of grace* look like in your life? And what relational rhythms could help you to behold God?

5

THE LOVE REFLEX

As we input the stimulus of God's love for
us, we reflex with love for others.

In Mark 12, a religious leader came to Jesus and asked him which of the commandments were the most important:

> 'The most important one,' answered Jesus, 'is this: "Hear, O Israel: the Lord our God, the Lord is one. Love the Lord your God with all your heart and with all your soul and with all your mind and with all your strength." The second is this: "Love your neighbour as yourself." There is no commandment greater than these.'
>
> Mark 12:29–31

We are commanded to love. To love God. And to love others.

Let me be honest with you. I find it somewhat problematic that we are *commanded* to love. As a parent I can demand that my kids put the bins out or empty the dishwasher, but can I really command them to love me? Surely we love what we love? How can love be a command? Is not love an expression of free will? Is not love an emotional response, a feeling that is either present or absent? Do we not *fall* in love?

Perhaps you, like me, have experienced the sort of situation where someone was in need; maybe they needed some help moving house, or paying a bill, or watching their kids. You knew you *should* help them, but it seemed so inconvenient, so much hassle, and you were *so* busy. And perhaps like me you left that situation feeling rubbish because it exposed your lack of love and compassion for others. *Jesus* would have loved them and met their need. But I just put my fingers in my ears, closed my eyes, and walked on by. We end up feeling guilty, a bad Christian.

God's Love Changes Everything

You'll discover that one of the heroes of this book is my mother, Joan. At the time of writing, she is in her eighties, still passionately loving Jesus and loving others. She's a tiny (4 foot 11), fiercely determined and outspoken follower of Jesus who has preached the gospel to me through her words and works all my life. Once a week, I take Mum out. I normally have a full English breakfast; she will have a mango and coconut smoothie, smoked salmon and poached eggs. She will give me the low-down on who said what, who has died, who she is not happy with. She will chat to the waitresses and anyone sat on the adjacent tables, all while dressed from head to toe in purple, including a purple rinse through her hair. After food, I have a walk around the city centre while Mum does her thing.

She will go from homeless person to homeless person giving them food and hot drinks. Often we meet up after half an hour or so, and she will be chatting to some homeless guy. She will introduce me to him, 'This is my son … he is a pastor.' Then she will give the homeless guy a hug – and then she will look at me with *that* look. The sort of look only a mother can give a son. A look that says, 'Now it's your turn to hug him.'[1]

Honestly, I struggle with that. I imagine many people would. To physically express love to someone you don't know and who has not had a bath or changed their clothes for months is not natural for most of us. I have talked to Mum about this on many occasions. Where does the love come from? You see, Mum would tell you that she doesn't find it easy. But she is compelled to act. For her, it's a reflex. And if you were to know her story, then you would see why.

My mum was born in Liverpool in 1935. She was abandoned by her parents at an early age and put into a convent to be 'cared for' by nuns. When the war broke out, Liverpool was seen as a target for Nazi bombing, so Mum, like many other children at the time, was sent to the countryside as an evacuee. She was put on a train, sent to a rural area, and met by her new 'family'. This is how my mum ended up in Yorkshire, at about the age of six. The family she lived with were pretty dysfunctional, and the 'care' she received – well, let's just say that by today's standards they would have probably been imprisoned. But it was not today; it was 1940s wartime Britain. She was kept off school and experienced emotional and physical abuse. Perhaps worst of all, she wasn't treated like a sibling in the home – she was 'Joan the evacuee'. There was little to no affection.

When my mum was about twelve, something incredible happened. Her 'step-brother', Henry,[2] was lying on the sofa waiting to die. He'd had tuberculosis and invasive surgery to remove two-thirds of one lung and more than one-third of the other. The letter box clicked, with a flyer advertising a 'healing crusade'. Mum was sent out of the house to find the people who had put the flyer through the letterbox. She brought them back to the house. They prayed for Henry, and he was instantly and completely healed. He went on to live a healthy life right through to his eighties, despite his reduced lung capacity.

Off the back of this, Mum started attending the local Pentecostal church. There she met a lady called Ellen, or Nell. Nell was the first person to ever hug Mum. Nell was the first person to ever buy my mum a birthday present – a bar of Toblerone chocolate. Nell loved my mum with the love of Jesus, and it transformed her life. Nell went on to live with Mum until the day Nell died, and I knew Nell as my gran.

For Mum, her relationship with Jesus changed everything. Quite literally everything. Imagine growing up believing you were unloved, unwanted, and then encountering Jesus, experiencing his embrace, and receiving his love *through* the love and embrace of one of his children (Nell). So, when Mum sees someone neglected or unloved, she reflexes with God's love for that person. She has an incredible spiritual radar for the adopted or fostered child within our church community. She will give them sweets and a smile. For her, it is as natural as blinking when poked in the eye. As she has received the love of God, she has been enabled to obey the command to love.

Beloved Children of God

In 1 John 4:19, we read these simple but profound words: 'We love because he first loved us.' This is the reflex. As we receive love, we reflex with love for others. So how do we input the love of God so that this reflex can occur?

The book of 1 John is all about love. In five relatively short chapters the words *love* or *loved* are mentioned forty times. And this ought not to surprise us, for John was the *beloved* disciple. He was the one who had experienced so much of Jesus' love, he was known as 'the one Jesus loved' (John 20:2). It was John who reclined beside Jesus at the Last Supper, and at the cross it was John who Jesus connected with his mother.[3] John absolutely knew his identity as loved. And so it follows that when time came to put pen to paper, it was John who called his followers to experience the love of the Father and to reflex with love for one another: 'See what great love the Father has lavished on us, that we should be called children of God! And that is what we are!' (1 John 3:1).

Did you notice that John used the word *see*? Look. Behold. It's the language of reflex. It's the *behold-believe-behave* journey of the reflex principle. As we see the love of God lavished upon us, we reflex with right identity. We see ourselves for who we really are, as beloved children of God. As we explored in the previous chapter, this is the power of beholding. This in turn always impacts our behaviour. There are some Christian traditions that emphasise contemplation. Perhaps this should be a priority for all children of God, for contemplation simply means the act of looking, from the Latin *contemplari* meaning *to gaze* or *to observe*. Richard Foster brilliantly captures this idea when he says, 'The contemplative life is the steady gaze of the soul upon the God who loves us.'[4]

As we gaze at God's love for us, demonstrated on the cross, we reflex with right identity as beloved children of God. And as we rest secure in that identity, our behaviour changes. Hurt people who hurt people become loved people who love people. Abandoned and rejected people find a home and invite others into that home. Such is the power of God's love to transform our lives.

One reflex outcome of God's love at work in the community of believers I am a part of is that many families foster and adopt. It is a natural response to God's love at work in their lives. After all, an ongoing encounter with the love of God always empowers us to love in bold, radical and risky ways. One of the champions of fostering within our community is the Atkinson family.[5] If you were to look at their family prior to their journey of fostering and adoption, you would have seen a family that had it all: well-paid, stable and meaningful jobs, a lovely home, two beautiful children of their own. And yet, as they have grown in the security of God's love for them, and as they have grown in their identity as God's children, they have opened up their home and their hearts to children who have found themselves in the care system, children often with nothing more than a black bin bag of possessions. As humans, we tend to instinctively work to make our lives easier and more comfortable. But fostering and adoption does not make life easier. Adopting a child with special needs has had a huge impact on the Atkinsons' time and energy. It has been an emotional rollercoaster. At times, it has derailed their plans and trashed their home. Fostering has not made their lives easier, but it has made their lives more rewarding, more transformational and more like Jesus. Their encounter with the love of God has empowered them to love others in a radical way. When their foster child took a pen and drew himself onto a family photograph, they knew God was leading them to adopt him fully into their family. It is a story that beautifully echoes the gospel.

A Gospel All About Love

The gospel is all about love. It's a gospel that starts with Father, Son and Spirit coexisting in loving union. This loving Trinity overflows with love in creating all things to love, culminating with humanity: the pinnacle of creation and the object of God's great affection. It's a gospel that flows through every page of Scripture, as God pursues his fallen, wayward creation in love. It's a gospel revealed in the Father sending the Son, such was the Father's love for the whole world.[6] And of course, it's a gospel ultimately hinging on the sacrificial love of the Son in giving his life for us. This gospel expresses itself continually in our lives, as we experience the power of a loving relationship with him from now to eternity. As such, you can't understand the gospel without love. You can't preach the gospel to yourself without reminding yourself of the love of God. Without love there is no motive, no reason *why*.

John, the beloved disciple, says,

> God is love. This is how God showed his love among us: he sent his one and only Son into the world that we might live through him. This is love: not that we loved God, but that he loved us and sent his Son as an atoning sacrifice for our sins. Dear friends, since God so loved us, we also ought to love one another.
>
> 1 John 4:8–11

God's very nature is love. As we behold him, as we gaze at him, we are transformed increasingly into his loving image. God's perfect love is demonstrated through sacrifice. As we consider the cross and try to get our heads around the Father sending the Son to suffer and die in our place, we too begin to overflow with love for those around us. It is not a love reserved for that which is beautiful or pleasing or has value. It is the sort of love that leads an elderly lady to hug the homeless. It is *God's* love.

When I think of my mum's story, it always reminds me of the story in Luke's Gospel, of the 'sinful woman' and her alabaster jar. Not because Mum lived that sort of life, but rather because both the 'sinful woman' and my mum were transformed by Christ's love and forgiveness. Their actions reflexed out of their encounter. Take a few moments to gospel yourself by reading the story right now in Luke 7:36–50.

It's a moving story. Jesus is at the house of one of the religious elite, Simon the Pharisee. They're enjoying a meal together with the wider extended family, as was their tradition. For Simon, this meal would have been an expression of religious duty. The food that was selected and the way it was prepared would have followed strict rules and regulations – all part of Simon's attempts to achieve righteousness. He wouldn't have wanted anyone or anything to defile this moment. And into his house – most probably full of servants, family members and guests – walks in a woman with a reputation. She has come prepared. She has a plan. We know this because she is carrying an alabaster jar of perfume. Both the jar and its contents would have been costly, about a year's worth of wages. We might think of it as her pension pot. She stands behind Jesus, most probably because he is reclined at the meal table. And she is weeping. She washes Jesus' feet with her tears. She dries them with her hair, kissing them. She breaks open her alabaster jar and pours it out and onto the feet of Jesus. Her encounter led to an outpouring. Her experience of Jesus reflexed with action. Her devotion stands in stark contrast to Simon's duty.

Simon secretly judges her for this, and judges Jesus for allowing it. So, Jesus responds with a story: one man owed a money lender five hundred days' wages; another man owed fifty days' wages. Neither could pay. Both had their debt cancelled.

Can you see the gospel message right there? Jesus asks Simon, 'Which of them will love the money lender more?' Simon replies, 'The one who had the bigger debt cancelled.' Herein lies the reflex. When our debt is paid and we receive the forgiveness of Jesus, we reflex with love. The more we understand how indebted we were, the more love we reflex. As Jesus says to Simon, 'Therefore, I tell you, her many sins have been forgiven – as her great love has shown. But whoever has been forgiven little loves little' (verse 47). The woman's outward actions demonstrated her inward reception of grace.

I don't know about you, but I find these words of Jesus deeply challenging. I find them challenging because to 'love little' is like a dull reflex, a delayed blink of the eye or a slow swing of the knee. Loving little is like a diagnostic that exposes the extent to which I am aware of God's forgiveness and grace at work in my life. If we take a look at the extent to which we show love to others, we can trace it back to the extent to which we are experiencing the reality of God's loving forgiveness in our own life. If we were to daily and deliberately spend time reflecting on our need for God's forgiveness, what might be the impact? If we were to daily contemplate the availability of that forgiveness and the newness of his mercy towards us each day, what effect would that have?[7] If we were to daily rejoice in his total, complete forgiveness of our sins *because of* his love for us, what would happen? I am pretty confident of this ... that the measure to which we input the weight of God's love for us is the measure with which we reflex with love for those around us. As Jesus said, we will either 'love little' or 'love more' depending on our encounter.

Love in Action

'To love is to act.' These are the words of Victor Hugo, author of *Les Misérables*, a story perhaps inspired by the 'sinful woman'. In *Les Mis,* the kind bishop Myriel extends grace and love to the convict Valjean, and the reflex is transformational. It's a salvation story, certainly inspired by the story of Jesus. And it's a story Hugo himself tried to live out as a renowned human rights activist in the 1800s, campaigning for free education for all children and an end to poverty. Such was his impact that he was awarded a state funeral, although he requested in his will a pauper's funeral, donating 50,000 francs to the poor. His final words? 'To love is to act.'[8]

> This is how we know what love is: Jesus Christ laid down his life for us. And we ought to lay down our lives for our brothers and sisters. If anyone has material possessions and sees a brother or sister in need but has no pity on them, how can the love of God be in that person? Dear children, let us not love with words or speech but with actions and in truth.
>
> 1 John 3:16–18

These verses capture the essence of the biblical concept of love, or *agape* – a sort of love that is expressed in costly action, like the sharing of material possessions with those in need. These words reflect the sort of life of love Jesus lived, and the death of love Jesus died.[9] They echo the words we read earlier from 1 John 4, that love calls us to action, to lay down our lives for others.

To love is to make a difference in the world, to bring heaven to earth, to advance God's kingdom. Jesus' miracles reflexed out of his love and compassion for the people. It was his love that led him to feed the hungry, give sight to the blind and raise the dead.[10] Martin Luther King Jr, the great civil rights activist, put it this way when he said, 'Love and justice are the same, for justice is love distributed, nothing else.'[11]

But what drives this love in action? Is it because I am overwhelmed by the needs of the world around me? Is it a response to feeling crushed by the weight of brokenness and inequality and poverty? Is it out of a sense that the solution to these things is to dig deep and get busy? As we know by now, the answer is a resounding *no*! These are the wrong types of stimuli; they are driven by the outcomes.

Instead, the reflex principle allows us to love others out of the overflow of God's love which we have received. It means it's not about how much money I give to the homeless or how many lasagnes I cook for my struggling neighbours. These things are not my primary concern. My primary concern is to receive and enjoy the love of God, to allow his love to shape my identity, knowing that my behaviour will naturally flow out of this. That is when our action flows out of the right heart, the right stimulus, the overflow of God's love. There is a subtle but powerful nuance here worth highlighting: *our* action flows out of *God's* love. That is so important. It is not flowing out of *my* love, for my love is finite and fleeting. My love comes and goes. It gets topped up and used up. One day I do something nice for someone because I am 'feeling it', but then the next day, when I am not 'feeling it', I am inactive. That's what happens when my actions are based on *my* love.

It seems to me that we can be serving at a food bank, giving to the poor, feeding and housing the homeless, expressing 'love through action', but it's the stimulus that put us there that makes all the difference. It can either be an attempt to earn the approval of God and others, an action dependent on our levels of love. Or it can be a natural reflex to the infilling love of God, an outcome of the gospel stimulus in our lives. Kingdom activity, as good and important as it is, usually, if not always, leads us into weariness, a loss of joy and ultimately burnout if it is not reflexing out of covenantal identity. We can become overwhelmed by the need, and feel that we have given out all the love we have. Our tank is empty.

As a church leader, I can often get trapped into the mindset of doing stuff for God. Not a problem if my *doing* for God is reflexing out of my *being* with God. But it is important, whatever our job, to remind ourselves that it is about God's love at work through us.

Church leaders often use the book of Nehemiah to preach on vision, strategy and building projects. One of the things I love about Nehemiah's building project and programmes of social transformation is that Nehemiah's work reflexed out of his relationship with God. Nehemiah's heart was broken for the people in the presence of God. This then reflexed with social action, to make a difference for those people on his heart, and ultimately the people on God's heart.[12]

How often do we hear of an issue and feel we must immediately respond with action? How often do we think that the best answer to someone's problems is for *us* to *do* something? Fix it now, fix it quick. Or maybe, as I described at the beginning of this chapter, you just avoid the crisis, bury your head in the sand and wait for the guilt to pass. Maybe you are great at fixing people's problems, but wonder why you get worn out and exhausted by the needs of others.

When Nehemiah heard of the suffering and brokenness of the people, this was his response, 'When I heard these things, I sat down and wept. For some days I mourned and fasted and prayed before the God of heaven' (Nehemiah 1:4). Nehemiah's first response to the need around him was to engage with God. For some days! It was a covenantal response. His desire for action was preceded by prayer. Nehemiah was basically saying, *God if you want me to do something about this, you are going to have to supernaturally make a way.*

> Lord, let your ear be attentive to the prayer of this your servant and to the prayer of your servants who delight in revering your name. Give your servant success today by granting him favour in the presence of this man. I was cupbearer to the king.
>
> Nehemiah 1:11

Nehemiah's action was placed entirely in God's hands. It was a reflex that came out of Nehemiah's time in God's presence. Interestingly, when building work finally started it was Eliashib the high priest and his fellow priests who were the first to start building.[13] The priests who regularly spent time in God's presence were the ones who were ready to act. I believe people of God's presence are always the first to truly impact the world around them. It is a false distinction to think that some people are called to worship and prayer, others to action. Sure, each of us will have a natural inclination to either covenant or kingdom, but both components are necessary for a healthy Christian life. However, as we've already noted, it has to start with covenant, with kingdom action reflexing out of relationship. This is God's pattern for the social transformation of the places we live. Don't just set up a food bank or homeless shelter. Press into the presence of God, capture his heart for the lost and broken and allow your loving deeds to reflex out of that.

Later on, Nehemiah and the building team were experiencing intimidation and fatigue. Nehemiah's response? Prayer.[14] To draw back into the presence of God. This is how we sustain love expressed through action. This is how we combat compassion fatigue. *Through intimacy.* For Nehemiah it was prayer and encounter that empowered him to press on with his project.

Maybe you are facing intimidation and fatigue in the places where you want to see kingdom breakthrough. Perhaps you are worn out by trying to do enough kingdom activity to solve the problems of the world. If that is your reality, the solution is not necessarily to stop all the kingdom activity, although the Father might call you to do that for a time. Rather, the solution is to press into the Father, to do the things that help you to encounter and behold his love, to abide more deeply in him; to remind yourself of the wonderful love of God demonstrated *for you* through the cross; to fill up your tank with his love. When we do this, our kingdom activity becomes sustainable; we have the rhythm to go the long haul. Just like in John 15, the branches naturally bear fruit when they abide in the Vine.

So, what will love lead you to build? Maybe it could lead you to build friendship with the stressed-out parent at the school gate or the difficult neighbour or the challenging colleague at work. For some, love has led them to build bridges into broken communities or create food banks for the recently unemployed. For others, love has led them further afield, to build orphanages in India or schools in the Congo. For the Atkinsons, it led them to build a bigger family. For my mum, love led her to building relationships with the homeless in Liverpool.

Whatever it is that love leads us to build, the key is to input the love of God; to receive the love of God and be sustained by the love of God. The secret is to behold. To contemplate. It is more than simply knowing about God's love. It is to see his love unfolding on every page of Scripture, and ultimately displayed on the cross; to experience his love warming our hearts, by his Holy Spirit; to taste of his love as we share bread and wine; to sing of his love as we wake and fall asleep; to hear his love, as he gently whispers our names. This is the stimulus, the input of God's love, that leads us to naturally reflex with love for God and love for our neighbour. It is the love of God that empowers us and enables us to fulfil his greatest of commands.

QUESTIONS FOR DISCUSSION

1. What prevents you from knowing how much you are
    loved by the Father?

2. What does it look like for you to input this love in your
    daily life?

3. What might love lead you to build?

6

THE JOY REFLEX

When we make happiness the goal, we are left unsatisfied.
When we behold Jesus, we reflex with joy.

Happiness is a big deal in today's society. The human quest seems to be the quest for happiness. There is something about being human, about simply living, that seems to make us aware that things are not as they ought to be; that there is more. This longing in the human heart, an awareness of something missing, is God-given, hardwired. It is there to lead us to God, the fountain of joy. Or, to put it in the words of C. S. Lewis, 'If we find ourselves with a desire that nothing in this world can satisfy, the most probable explanation is that we were made for another world.'[1]

But that does not stop people from trying to find happiness in all manner of things. The search for happiness has become a big industry. It is fundamentally how sales and advertising work. Advertising tells us that we have a need, we are miserable, and if we buy that thing, whether that be a car, or a burger, or an experience, then we will be happy. The 2006 film *The Pursuit of Happyness* plays on this idea, what we might call *the American Dream*. It explores the battles of a failing salesman, played brilliantly by Will Smith, who struggles to make ends meet selling bone scanners. In the end, he randomly secures a high-paid job and goes on to form his own multimillion-dollar brokerage firm. It's a rags-to-riches story, a theme that runs through so many stories. And yet, the idea that happiness lies just around the corner, something you might attain one day, is such a poor story compared to the glorious gospel story. The gospel is good news because it means *right now*, whatever circumstances you face in life, you can be joyful as you learn to keep your gaze fixed on Jesus.

Interestingly, the phrase *the pursuit of happiness* originates from the American Declaration of Independence, which states, 'We hold these truths to be self-evident, that all men are created equal, that they are endowed by their Creator with certain unalienable Rights, that among these are Life, Liberty and the pursuit of Happiness.'

Deep in our psyche lies this idea that happiness is a human right; it is on a par with human equality, the right to life and the right to freedom. But is our right to happiness valid? The American founding fathers thought it was not only valid but true and self-evident. And I am inclined to agree with them.

God wants you to be happy. But he wants you to be happy as *he* defines happiness, not as the world defines it. We have watered down happiness. We have made it into a temporary mood, a shallow emotion or passing feeling. But happiness as God defines it is far more than feeling perky or chipper. Happiness is our eternal destiny. Why? Because heaven is our home. As C. S. Lewis says, 'Joy is the serious business of heaven.'² Joy is the purest form of happiness, and experiencing heaven's joy is part of our mandate and calling as Christians to bring heaven to earth.

Perhaps the best word we have in the Bible for happiness is the word *blessed*. Blessed is the Greek word *makarios*, and *makarios* is a big word. If you smiled then, well done for getting my theological joke. If you didn't get it, then don't worry, it means you are normal! The prefix of *makarios* is *mak* from which we get the word *macro*, which means *to enlarge* or *make bigger*, hence 'a big word'. But as they say with jokes, if you have to explain it, it is not a joke. Anyway, *makarios* carries with it a sense of God enlarging you, making you bigger – spiritually, of course, although in the ancient Near East getting physically bigger would have been an indication of being blessed because it meant you had an abundance of food and wine!

One of the ways of translating *makarios* is like this: *congratulations are in order*. So, for example, if someone got engaged to be married – *makarios*! Congratulations are in order. Life is about to get a whole lot bigger. And so there is this sense in being *blessed* that we receive something now that guarantees something to come … like engagement. Engagement is not the goal, it is not complete in and of itself. Engagement is a taste, a glimpse of the marriage that is to come. But when someone gets engaged they will feel blessed, happy. Why? Because they have secured something in the here and now that guarantees something bigger in the future. Or we might think of paying for a summer holiday in the winter … how do you feel when you do that? Excited! Happy! Blessed! You have stepped into something in the here and now that guarantees something bigger in the future. Blessed. *Makarios*. Being made bigger. Happiness. Satisfaction. Congratulations are in order.

True blessing here and now is a foretaste of our eternal destiny. That blessing will intensify your desire for your future inheritance, as receiving a ring might intensify one's desire for marriage. It reassures us in the waiting. We might not have the full experience of what is to come right now, but we have the guarantee, the down payment, the deposit of God's Spirit within us, that stirs longing and excitement and confidence in what will surely come.[3]

Of course, when we input the gospel into our lives – reminding ourselves of what God has already done for us in adopting us into his family and filling us with his Spirit – it stirs something inside us. We feel blessed. Content. Joyful. Even when our circumstances don't look blessed by the world's standards, we know we are blessed, because we experience Jesus living within us. We experience here and now a foretaste of our eternal and guaranteed destiny.

It is widely believed that it was Corrie ten Boom who said, 'You can never learn that Christ is all you need, until Christ is all you have.'[4] The reason these words ring true with such power is that Corrie ten Boom said them while in a Nazi concentration camp during the Second World War, where she was imprisoned for hiding Jews. Even in that place, she was blessed. Why? Because she had Jesus.

But we seem to easily forget this simple truth.

The Happiness Myth

Do a quick google search, and you will find no shortage of voices telling you how to achieve happiness. I call this the *happiness myth*; compelling stories of how to be happy. They are compelling because, as with all myths, they are based on a seed of truth. The kernel of truth is something like this: we were made to experience happiness. So, the pursuit of happiness is natural, instinctive. But ultimately, these myths leave us disappointed and unsatisfied. This is because myths take a seed of truth and then wrap that truth in layers and layers of falsehood and fantasy. The kernel of truth gets wrapped in layers of Disney and Hollywood. Let me give you a few examples.

The myth that *if I get the right job, then I will be happy.* There is so much truth in this myth, which is why it is so powerful. Work is indeed good and rewarding. But work, in and of itself, can't give you true or lasting happiness. Or the myth that *finding mister or missus right will make me happy.* Again, the truth in this myth is that 'It is not good for man to be alone' (Genesis 2:18), that relationships are a gift from God for human flourishing; they bring joy into our lives. But another human cannot bring you true or lasting happiness. Or the myth that *rest will make me happy.* If I can only remove all pressure and hardship from my life and achieve some meditative Zen-like state, then I will be happy. Once again, rest is good and God-given. Without it, there is no happiness. But true rest comes through abiding in Christ.

One big myth I've personally had to unravel over the years is the myth that if *I buy x, y or z, then I will be happy.* My wife and friends joke that I have a garage full of past-hobbies. All the gear, no idea. Road bikes. Beer brewing equipment. A homemade meat-curing fridge. Mountain climbing stuff. I have a tendency to move from fad to fad in the pursuit of fulfilment, although I like to think it is more to do with my apostolic, pioneering gifting. But let us call it what it really is: *consumerism* – one of the most compelling of all myths. If, like me, you struggle with this myth, I would suggest you will never really break free from it until you can identify and acknowledge the seed of truth at the heart of it. It will require coming face to face with the gnawing lack of satisfaction in your heart; and putting 'stuff' into its rightful place and naming it for what it is. If 'stuff' sits in the place of God, it is an idol. And what we behold, we worship. If we make the things we own the objects of our affection, we reflex by living our lives orientated around them. Our purpose in life becomes determined by having the things we want. Our sense of security, wellbeing and value as a person becomes defined by whether we own the right things. But idols can never satisfy in the way that God can; they can't fill us with true happiness. We can amass all the shiny stuff in the world and still feel empty. We discover there is no pot of treasure at the end of the rainbow.

Although consumerism and the pursuit of stuff is very much part of the 'spirit of the age', it's not actually a modern phenomenon. It is an aspect of fallen human nature. It is how we are wired. It echoes back to the ancient world, to King Solomon, the wealthiest man of his generation who said these incredibly sad words, 'Yet when I surveyed all that my hands had done and what I had toiled to achieve, everything was meaningless, a chasing after the wind; nothing was gained under the sun' (Ecclesiastes 2:11).

All his accomplishments, all his possessions and experiences – in the end it was all meaningless. Empty. Vapid. This is the happiness myth.

Good Advice vs Good News

There is so much 'good advice' out there as to how to achieve happiness. But we are not good-advice people. We are good-news people. And the gospel speaks of a better way. The problem starts when we make the wrong thing our goal. This is why beholding speaks so powerfully into the happiness myth. If you make the pursuit of happiness your goal, I guarantee you will reflex with feeling miserable and disappointed. But if you make the pursuit of beholding Jesus your goal, you will reflex with pure and lasting joy. Joy is found in his presence. As the psalmist says, 'You make known to me the path of life; you will fill me with joy in your presence, with eternal pleasures at your right hand' (Psalm 16:11).

The church is not exempt from thinking we should pursue happiness. Christians seem to lack no immunity to happiness myths. Sure, we know that satisfaction, peace and joy are found in relationship with God. When we return to our Creator, we find rest and happiness. We most probably discovered this when we first responded to the gospel and gave our lives to Jesus. Much like the reflex of joy experienced by a child unwrapping gifts at Christmas, as we first began to unwrap the great gift of salvation, of sins forgiven, conscience cleansed, relationship restored – oh what joy filled our hearts! But then gospel amnesia crept in. We forgot how good the good news is and started looking for our sense of happiness and wellbeing elsewhere. We drifted.

Over time, many of us trade the good news of Jesus with what a church leader friend of mine calls *therapeutic Christianity*. We begin to view church, the gathering of believers, in the same way we view the gym or the shops. We think, *I am not feeling happy, I will go to church, that will cheer me up.* It's a bit like hitting the gym if we are feeling flabby or heading to the shops for some retail therapy. I hope that meeting with other believers *does* give you a little boost, because it is good to have the habit of meeting with other believers.[5] I hope in your church community you hear the gospel proclaimed through the songs, through the reading of Scriptures and through the sharing of bread and wine. And I hope attending church is a place where you look to serve and give to others, as well as being a place where you receive. But the real impact of attending church is not attending a meeting when we need a pick-me-up. The real impact happens when attending church becomes one of our many regular rhythms of devotion. For me, going to church on a Sunday but having no regular rhythm of devotion is a bit like going for an all-you-can-eat buffet when you've been living on bread and water all week. It might feel good at the time and satisfy you in the moment, but it won't nourish you in a way that will sustain you to reflex into all of the kingdom opportunities you have for the following week. What we need is a regular intake of nourishing food, then Sunday becomes the weekly feast-gathering with fellow believers – an opportunity to bless and serve one another, to share and celebrate all that God is doing among us.

There is, I believe, another version of therapeutic Christianity creeping into the church. It is a mix of Christianity and the self-care movement.[6] Again, as with all myths, it starts with a seed of truth. God wants you to love and care for yourself. After all, you can't love your neighbour if you don't love yourself. True. But it is in the outworking of this truth that we come unstuck. How do we love and care for ourselves more? By going on holiday and sunning ourselves on the beach? By treating ourselves to a takeaway on a Friday night? Maybe through gym membership or a monthly massage and spa treatment? No, true self-care happens when we grow in love and care for ourselves through intimacy with God as we input the gospel, as we gaze at Jesus. All the things we might do to care for ourselves are not necessarily negative, but they are only fruitful if they are ways of making space for more of Jesus. So, when I go on a mountain walk, I do so to encounter Jesus. When I go for a swim and sauna at the gym, I find it a really healthy way to, 'Cast my cares onto Jesus because he cares for me' (my paraphrase of 1 Peter 5:7). As I walk the dog I pray in tongues, because I know, 'Praying in the Spirit builds me up in the most holy faith' (my paraphrase of Jude 1:20). I find happiness through all sorts of counter-intuitive practices. It's about choosing the right stimulus.

Jesus magnificently unpacks this paradoxical kind of blessing for us in Matthew 5 in what is known as *The Beatitudes*.[7] When we read the word *blessed* in this passage, we need to read it as *happy as God defines happiness*. When we read it this way, being blessed is about the satisfaction and joy that is found in him; that is not only to come (like the wedding) but impacts our here and now (like the engagement ring). Take some time to read it now in Matthew 5:1–12.

Let me draw out two aspects of happiness from this remarkable passage. First, we are blessed when we are poor in spirit (verse 3). It seems so upside down and counter-intuitive that we might experience blessing – happiness – through some sort of lack. Happy are the poor. How can that be? When American pastor and preacher A. W. Tozer unpacked this verse, he talked about the *tyranny of stuff*. The poor in spirit are those who have freed themselves from the tyranny and oppression of possessions. They have broken the hold of consumerism, or to use the words of Jesus in the parable of the sower, they have loosened the stranglehold of 'the worries of this life and the deceitfulness of wealth' that choke the seed of the gospel (Matthew 13:22).

I have already confessed to struggling with consumerism, although it would be true to say that this struggle only crept into my life as an adult. As a child growing up in a single-parent family, we had very little. In fact, one of my earliest memories is sitting hungrily at the dining room table and praying with my mum for food because the cupboards were bare. The doorbell rang, and there on the doorstep was a bag of shopping. Although I was aware as a child that most of my clothes and toys were second-hand, I only ever felt a sense of satisfaction for them, a sense of gratitude and appreciation towards God for them. But at some point later in life, ever so gradually, the consumerism crept in.

One of the things God has used to help me experience breakthrough from the tyranny of stuff has been spending time in some of the poorest communities in the world, in places such as the Democratic Republic of Congo, and parts of India. In those places I've encountered beautiful Christians who materially have so little and yet are so rich in God's blessing. They are blessed. Why? Because they have Jesus. Or rather, the challenges of daily life have forced them to keep their gaze fixed on Jesus, to find contentment in Jesus. And their example has helped me to reconnect to that sense of gratitude towards God that I experienced as a child.

But the idea of blessing reflexing out of a poverty of spirit runs even deeper than freedom from consumerism. It is an idea embedded in the very essence of what it means to be a disciple. There is a cost to being a disciple of Jesus. There is a denying of self. Following Jesus is a call to lay something down, to surrender. We might therefore think of discipleship as a 'poverty'. And as we engage in that process, we find we reflex with joy. We are blessed. This ought not to surprise us, for Jesus clearly connected the outcome of joy with the sort of obedience that reflexes out of love.

> If you keep my commands, you will remain in my love, just as I have kept my Father's commands and remain in his love. I have told you this so that my joy may be in you and that your joy may be complete.
>
> John 15:10–11

On my desk at work, I have a precious gift. It is a sachet of instant coffee, probably worth a couple of pence. But I won't open it, and it sits on my office desk as a reminder of its owner. If you look carefully at it, you will see the lettering is Korean. It was given to me by a little elderly North Korean lady called Wing Lei, who wanted to give a gift of coffee to everyone she met.[8] Wing Lei was a leader in the secret and persecuted church in North Korea. For many years, she was imprisoned in a labour camp for being a follower of Jesus. She was forced to sleep on a freezing-cold concrete floor, given very little food and made to work incredibly hard. She was regularly beaten. And yet, in that camp, she started a secret church. She would tell people about Jesus. They would sync toilet breaks and meet in the toilets for just a few minutes, several times a day, to pray and worship Jesus. Eventually, Wing Lei was released and was able to make the dangerous journey across the border to South Korea. If you were to meet Wing Lei, the first thing you would notice is her smile. She is full of the joy of the Lord. She is blessed. She has Jesus. Happy are the poor in spirit, for theirs is the kingdom of heaven.

Shortly before Christmas one year, I read something that immensely challenged me and impacted my tradition of

Christmas excessiveness. It may well also have saved my waist-
line. I was reading about the early Amish, Quaker, Mennonite
and Anabaptist communities of the late sixteenth and early
seventeenth centuries. These groups of Christians were given
the disparaging nickname of *plain folk* or *plain people* because
of the way they chose to dress. At a time when society and
the established church were so lavish and excessive, these
Christian communities decided to live and dress as plainly as
possible. They didn't make a song or dance about it; they just
did it. But society and the established church, obsessed with
acquiring wealth, found these plain folk so challenging that
they persecuted them. Many were attacked, imprisoned, even
burned at the stake. And yet in those days, the gospel spread
and society was transformed. Plain folk. People who found
happiness in being freed from the tyranny of stuff. Blessed are
the poor in spirit. I think we can learn a lot about happiness
from their way of life. It is easy to look back at these sorts of
movements in a romanticised way, as an almost 'return to the
good life' escape from the trappings of the world, much like a
corporate banker today might give it all up for a simpler life in
the country. But for these plain folk, it was more about remov-
ing the shiny things that charmed them in order to gaze more
steadily upon Jesus.

The second beatitude worth considering in relation to
happiness is found in Matthew 5:4, 'Blessed are those who
mourn, for they will be comforted.' Once again, this seems so
contradictory, so paradoxical. How can there be blessing for
those who mourn? Well, I don't think Jesus was talking about
putting on a fake smile while grieving. I don't believe Jesus
was suggesting we should pretend to be OK when we are not.
I find great comfort in the fact that Jesus himself experienced

grief. When Jesus arrived at his friend Lazarus' tomb, he wept.[9] He wept the sort of tears associated with extreme grief. When we read that Jesus was 'deeply moved in spirit' at Mary's tears, the Greek word is *embrimaomai*, meaning a *thundering of the spirit*.[10] It is the same word used for the snorting of a horse! It is that sort of visceral, extreme outcry we might experience when we hear of the death of a loved one. Not only did this grief fulfil Isaiah's prophecy of Jesus as the Messiah, a 'Man of sorrows and acquainted with grief',[11] but his tears and grief affirmed and dignified the tears of us all. Through his tears, Jesus demonstrated that there is no sin or shame or weakness in crying. Jesus experienced the whole breadth and depth of human emotion. So, we have to understand, in our imitation of Jesus, how being 'blessed' fits with the whole spectrum of human emotion.

The Covid-19 lockdowns presented us with many challenges, from acquiring loo roll, through to working from home via Zoom while simultaneously trying to homeschool the kids. There were those who lost loved ones, those whose business suffered, those who faced long-term financial uncertainty. There were those who had to survive in dangerous and abusive home environments.

Undoubtedly the pandemic placed a huge stress upon us all. I would say one of the dominant emotions we experienced in our common humanity was grief. Grief is the distress we experience through loss. It is a form of mourning. We grieved the loss of personal freedom and autonomy. Perhaps we grieved the loss of relationship, or holiday, or income, or health. There are clearly those who grieved because of death. And others grieved the security and satisfaction they derived from their work.

Yet Jesus' promise to us, in those times and now, is that we are blessed. It seems impossible, it seems like paradox, but it is an opportunity for blessing. Why? Because in the stripping away of all the things that have brought us comfort, we find a truer, purer comfort in Jesus. Blessed are those who mourn.

The Laughing Liberator

Jesus wept. And yet Jesus was and is the most joyful being in the universe. The writer to the Hebrews reminds us this,

> But about the Son he says, 'Your throne, O God, will last for ever and ever; a sceptre of justice will be the sceptre of your kingdom. You have loved righteousness and hated wickedness; therefore God, your God, has set you above your companions by anointing you with the oil of joy.'
>
> Hebrews 1:8–9

The anointing Jesus received was an anointing of joy. The oil of gladness was poured over Jesus. It is what set him apart from all others. The Greek word for joy here is *agalliasis* – wild, ecstatic delight and exhilaration. The passage is about Christ's throne. His kingdom. So, joy is a mark of the kingdom. The kingdom of heaven coming to earth includes heaven's joy being established on earth. It was the pursuit of this joy that empowered Jesus to endure the suffering of the cross.[12] Jesus knew the sort of joy that would be established for us in this new kingdom, and he considered the journey of suffering through the cross to be worth it. Paul echoes this when he says, 'For the kingdom of God is not a matter of eating and drinking, but of righteousness, peace and joy in the Holy Spirit' (Romans 14:17).

When I was a schoolteacher, one of my favourite lessons on the Religious Studies curriculum was a lesson for Year 7 (eleven- to twelve-year-olds) based on famous paintings of Jesus. In the lesson we showed a number of images of Jesus, and the pupils would describe the image as a way of forming theology about who Jesus is … a sort of Christology for kids. The images included famous paintings such as the 1853 oil on canvas *The Light of the World* by Holman Hunt, and Salvador Dalí's 1951 *Christ of Saint John of the Cross*. But the image that often caused the greatest positive reaction and learning was the lesser-known image created in 1973 by Canadian artist Willis Wheatley called *The Laughing Liberator*.[13] I would encourage you to google it right now. It is a simple pencil sketch of Jesus throwing his head back, with a huge smile on his face, perhaps laughing or maybe singing as he sets the captives free. This is who Jesus is. Jesus *is* the Laughing Liberator. Jesus is joy.

The church I lead in Liverpool planted a church in Greece a number of years ago, so we often visit the church and enjoy good relationships with the local Greek emerging leaders. We eat amazing Greek food. We enjoy the Greek vistas of mountains and beaches. And we laugh. A lot. One of the favourite things to laugh at is the way I pronounce Greek words. When preaching in the church, I might reference a New Testament Greek word like *oikos* or *eucharisteo*, but you can guarantee that none of the local Greeks understand what I'm saying, because I say it with such a strong Yorkshire accent. So, we often end up in discussions around the origins of Greek words. On a recent trip, I was talking about the Greek word for joy, *agalliasis*. And one of the local leaders explained that it was used to describe the emotional response to gazing at a statue of a Greek god. The ancient Greeks would behold a statue of a deity like Zeus or Aphrodite, and they would be overwhelmed with joy.

This is just like our reflex process. We behold, and we reflex with joy. For the Christian, joy is not a requirement. It is a consequence. An outcome. As we behold the face of Jesus, we reflex with joy. We see this idea throughout Scripture.

Psalm 16:8–11 says,

> I keep my eyes always on the LORD. With him at my right hand, I shall not be shaken. Therefore my heart is glad and my tongue rejoices; my body also will rest secure, because you will not abandon me to the realm of the dead, nor will you let your faithful one see decay. You make known to me the path of life; you will fill me with joy in your presence, with eternal pleasures at your right hand.

And again, in Isaiah 60:4–5:

> Lift up your eyes and look about you: all assemble and come to you; your sons come from afar, and your daughters are carried on the hip. Then you will look and be radiant, your heart will throb and swell with joy …

Look. See. Behold. And reflex with joy.

In Matthew 11, we read that John the Baptist was in prison. Now that would have been a pretty unhappy, joyless place to be. John sent two of his disciples to ask Jesus, 'Are you the one who is to come, or should we expect someone else?' (verse 3). I always find this a bit unexpected. It seems almost out of character for Jesus' cousin John, the famous baptiser in the desert, to be questioning whether Jesus is really the Messiah. But I think there is something deeper going on here. John had chosen to focus on what Jesus *had not done*, rather than on what he had done. John knew from the Old Testament prophecies that Jesus would set the captives free.[14] But Jesus had not delivered on that for John. No wonder John was disappointed. Doubting. He had not experienced that promise in his own life.

Jesus responds by pointing to what *is* happening, 'the blind receive sight, the lame walk, those who have leprosy are cleansed, the deaf hear, the dead are raised, and the good news is proclaimed to the poor' (verse 5). He called John to take his eyes off what Jesus had not done, and see what he *had* done. We all have times when we question or forget the good news of what Jesus is doing around us and in our lives … gospel amnesia. But Jesus calls us to look at what he *has done* and *is* doing. We have to behold right in order to believe and therefore behave right. It is a principle we can all put into practice. Start to see what Jesus has already done in your life. In other words, gospel yourself, and you will reflex with happiness. Jesus immediately goes on to say of John, 'Blessed is anyone who does not stumble [take offence or fall away] on account of me' (verse 6, brackets mine). Why is that important? It is important because, according to Jesus, you can be blessed in a prison cell! *Makarios*, happiness, is far less to do with our context and surroundings, and far more to do with our ability to recognise the work of Jesus in our lives.

Maybe you feel like you are in a prison right now. You feel trapped, surrounded by darkness. Your joy has gone. You are focusing on what Jesus has not done, the disappointment, the lack. Maybe freedom is just around the corner; the Laughing Liberator will release you from that captivity, and you will experience overwhelming joy, just as those exiles did when released from Babylon:

> When the LORD brought back the captive ones of Zion,
> We were like those who dream.
> Then our mouth was filled with laughter
> And our tongue with joyful shouting;
> Then they said among the nations,
> 'The LORD has done great things for them.'
> The LORD has done great things for us;
> We are joyful.
>
> Psalm 126:1–3 NASB

Maybe you will have that sort of breakthrough. I pray you will. Or maybe, like John the Baptist or like the apostle Paul, your story will end in hardship. Either way, you can still know God's joy. Joy can be yours. Why? Because you know Jesus. You can look to him. And he has freed us from a greater bondage. We have been set free from the slavery of sin and the bondage of death. How our mouths are filled with laughter and salvation songs when we input the stimulus of the gospel and remind ourselves of the victory of the cross and empty grave! Whatever our context, we will reflex with joy.

So, let me finish by saying something that might seem to negate what I said earlier in this chapter. Right at the offset, I said that if you pursue happiness, you will end up disappointed. You can't make joy and happiness the goal. I am now going to contradict that. Because, God is the happy God.[15] Jesus is pure joy. So, in that sense, pursuing happiness and joy is exactly what we should be doing, because the true pursuit of happiness is the pursuit of Christ. This is a truth that C. S. Lewis explores in his 1942 essay 'The Weight of Glory', in which he says,

> It would seem that Our Lord finds our desires not too strong, but too weak. We are half-hearted creatures, fooling about with drink and sex and ambition when infinite joy is offered us, like an ignorant child who wants to go on making mud pies in a slum because he cannot imagine what is meant by the offer of a holiday at the sea. We are far too easily pleased.[16]

Any pursuit of earthly joy, happiness or pleasure is like splashing around in a muddy puddle when a glorious sandy beach is just around the corner. Behold him. Delight in him. Savour and feast on him. And reflex with his joy in abundance in your life.

QUESTIONS FOR DISCUSSION

1. What happiness myths do we tend to believe, and what impact do they have on us?

2. What things do you have in your life right now that God has given to bring you joy?

3. In what ways could your self-care practices be empowered by the gospel?

7

THE GENEROSITY REFLEX

As we input the stimulus of an extravagant
gospel, we reflex with generosity.

Here is a confession for you. I have always struggled to be generous. I'm more naturally inclined to be mean, frugal and penny-pinching … a bit of a scrooge. Ask my kids and they'll tell you I don't go shopping, I go bargain hunting. They have been well trained to know that there is no point asking for something in the shops if it's not reduced and in the sale by at least 50 per cent! I think I learnt this behaviour from my mum, who has a keen eye for a bargain. Other than indulging in new hobbies, as I mentioned in the previous chapter, I'm pretty frugal. When a salesperson tells me they can save me money on my utility bills, I'm sure before they even go into the details that they can't, because I have already taken great delight in saving money on my utilities, as if it is some sort of sporting competition. Perhaps my frugality comes from being a Yorkshireman – we do have a reputation for being tight with our money. It is said that a Yorkshireman is like a Scotsman with the generosity squeezed out of him. More likely, it is probably because I grew up with so little, and if you too have experienced that, you will know it makes you more inclined to hold tightly onto what you have.

Whatever the cause or origin, it stands in stark contrast with the extravagant, generous God in whose image we have been made. As Psalm 84:11 says, 'no good thing does he withhold from those whose way of life is blameless'. Our generous Father in heaven has withheld no good thing from us – not even his own Son. That is surely the definition of generosity.

Kickstarting Generosity

If you have been a Christian any length of time or if you have ever attended a church, then you will know that an element of gathering together is that we are asked for money. Taking up the tithes and offerings is a pretty standard part of any church service. In the past this often brought up emotions of both guilt and fear. Guilt because I knew I should give some of my money to God. After all, he had done so much for me. Fear because of the basic maths of it. If I gave away some of what I had, I would have less. It does not take a maths genius to work that out. I was focused on my lack. Despite that, I still gave and have tithed since the days of getting pocket money as a kid. The difference nowadays is that it is a joy and delight for me to tithe to my local church. It excites me. This is because it reflexes out of my intimacy with Jesus. As I've said previously, you can have two people doing exactly the same thing; for one it is dutiful religious practice that leads to weariness; for the other it is joyful delight. The difference is that for the latter, the action is reflexing out of intimacy and devotion. It is the overflow. Generous giving is the natural reflex to the stimulus of preaching the gospel to oneself, because in the gospel we see displayed the incredible extravagance and generosity of God.

As a church leader, I now find myself in the position of asking my congregation for money. I preach on giving. I believe tithing is an entry-level access point to financial generosity, not because the church needs your money, but rather because we as individuals need to give. Giving transforms the giver. I don't find it easy to talk about money. In fact, for a long time I would feel nervously sick inside at the thought of making that ask of people. After all, what if it meant they didn't have enough money left to feed the kids or pay the bills? You can see how that sort of thinking reflexes out of a wrong understanding of God.

As a shepherd of God's flock, I am compelled to create opportunities for people to give. Someone once said to me after a church service in which I had preached on generosity, 'John, you are always talking about money.' I said, 'Thank you.' That is absolutely true. I don't think they meant it as a compliment, but I took it as one. I went on to explain that if I was talking about money, then I was talking about the things that Jesus talked about, and my goal in life was to be like Jesus.

Money was one of the main themes of Jesus' teaching. He had far more to say about money than prayer or Satan, for example. Depending on how you count it, maybe as many as one in ten verses in the Gospels are about money, wealth or giving. And that ought not to surprise us. The real issue here is Lordship. It is about how we live a life of devotion to God, how we live a life of surrender. Remember, the effort of grace is surrender. As a church leader, I can't really call people into the joyful freedom of surrender without challenging them to look at how they use their money and calling them to surrender their wallets, purses and bank accounts to Jesus. After all, as Jesus said, 'No one can serve two masters. Either you will hate the one and love the other, or you will be devoted to the one and despise the other. You cannot serve both God and Money' (Matthew 6:24).

There are a few things I find absolutely fascinating about that verse. First, it follows verse 22, which says, 'The eye is the lamp of the body' – words we considered in the chapter on the holiness reflex. So, these words on money in verse 24 relate to the concept of beholding, of what we look at. The verse is set in the context of worship or idolatry. Second, and following on from that, the word *money* here is the Greek word *Mammon*. Mammon was the Babylonian deity of money. Money person-ified. The idol of money. Jesus is saying you are either under God's Lordship or Mammon's lordship. There is no neutral ground. One will be your master. So somehow we have to find a way of bringing our finances under the Lordship of Jesus.

I take a very pragmatic view on how to do that. For me, I can think of no better way of breaking the power and hold of Mammon over our lives and bringing our finances under the Lordship of Christ than through tithing. Tithing is the giv-ing of our first 10 per cent to God, through the local church. Now, this is really important to say: *tithing is not generos-ity*. Tithing is recognising that all we have is God's, and as a way of acknowledging that it *all* belongs to him, we give him the first 10 per cent back. Tithing is either a dutiful obliga-tion or a joyful reflex to the generosity of God. But it is not generosity. To consider tithing as generous is a bit like going to a restaurant, eating the food, paying the bill, and thinking you have been generous for paying for the meal you have eaten! Generosity is like the tip – it is what is given above and beyond what is due.

So why talk about tithing or use it as a reflex example? Simply because I have never, ever, ever encountered a believer who stepped into abundant generosity far above their tithe who hadn't first experienced the tithe as a springboard into generosity. Tithing is like the bicycle stabilisers of generosity. It helps us to get started on the journey of generosity and to develop the confidence to be outrageous in our giving. Tithing helps us to put money in its rightful place and God in his rightful place. It helps us to acknowledge God as the giver of all things and that our money, along with the rest of our lives, belongs to him. It develops confidence because, through it, we test and prove God to be faithful to us in our finances, as we learn to bring our finances under his Lordship.

An Extravagant Father

Generosity is not just about our money. We see the many different facets of generosity when we begin to truly behold the extravagant, abundant Father we have. Our Father God is a 'Prodigal God', as Timothy Keller writes in his book of the same name.[1] Prodigal is simply an old English word from a Latin root meaning *lavish*, *extravagant* or *excessive*. No matter how excessive the prodigal son was in the parable, the Father was more so. His love, mercy and grace towards his wayward son truly was outrageously lavish and underserved. When I look across the story of God's people throughout the Bible, I continuously see the generous nature of God towards his people. I see that God is a God who wants to bless us abundantly. God is a God who wants all of his people to prosper and thrive. I see a God who is supremely concerned with the poor, calling his people to make provision for them.[2] God is generous. And the key to developing generous *behaviour* is to *behold* the generous One. When we focus on our lack and on what we don't have, then we hold onto the little we *do* have out of fear. Like John the Baptist, questioning whether Jesus was really the Messiah and focusing on what had not yet happened, we miss what God is doing and the opportunity to behold who he really is.[3] But when we feed on the gospel, when we preach it to our souls, we start to see the extravagant generosity of God in the salvation story, and we reflex with generosity to those around us.

We also see the generosity of God in creation. God makes a world in his image. All he has created is good. It is beautiful, complex and varied. It is abundant, overflowing and teeming with life. Not one kind of plant. Not one kind of fish or animal. But a mind-boggling variety. Over one million species of insect, 400,000 species of flowers, 300,000 species of edible plant, and stars and galaxies that are too numerous to count.[4] I don't think it is a stretch too far to say that God's abundance in the act of creation reflexed out of his abundant nature, out of who he is: identity reflexing with activity. And if you think about it, part of God's purpose in this was to create something for our enjoyment. For you and me. God did not need to create, for God existed before his creation in perfect fulfilment and lack of need. Rather, he created it all as a generous gift for humanity that would reveal his generous nature. He created so that we could enjoy him through it.

So, in a sense, how can we be generous towards God when it is all his anyway? How can you give to God of what he has already created?

C. S. Lewis brilliantly captures this idea in *Mere Christianity* when he says,

> Every faculty you have, your power of thinking or of moving your limbs from moment to moment, is given you by God. If you devoted every moment of your whole life exclusively to His service you could not give Him anything that was not in a sense His own already. So that when we talk of a man doing anything for God or giving anything to God, I will tell you what that is really like. It is like a small child going to its father and saying, 'Daddy, give me sixpence to buy you a birthday present.' Of course, the father does, and he is pleased with the child's present. It is all very nice and proper, but only an idiot would think that the father is sixpence to the good on the transaction. When a man has made these two discoveries God can really get to work. It is after this that real life begins. The man is awake now.[5]

This idea of giving back to God what he has already generously provided is captured by King David in 1 Chronicles 29. David's desire was to build a temple for God, and so he gave of his resources. He gave vast amounts of gold, silver, bronze, iron, wood and precious stones.[6] The value must have been enormous. And yet King David recognised he was only giving back to God from what God had given him. In verse 14, David prays, 'But who am I, and who are my people, that we should be able to give as generously as this? Everything comes from you, and we have given you only what comes from your hand.' And in verse 16, 'LORD our God, all this abundance that we have provided for building you a temple for your Holy Name comes from your hand, and all of it belongs to you.'

David, the worshipper, the man after God's own heart,[7] once a humble shepherd now a mighty king, reflexed with generosity to the generosity of God that he had experienced.

When my eldest son, Soren, hit his teenage years, he started going along to one of our church youth groups. As anyone who has ever gone to a church youth group will know, one of the big draws in your early teens is the tuck shop. Soren would happily sit through any length of sermon, no matter how boring, if armed with enough sweets, crisps and fizzy drinks. So, each Friday, we would give him a couple of pounds. On one occasion, we had no small change to give him, so we ended up having to trust him with a large note, £20, under strict instructions to bring home the change. Off Soren went to the youth group, arriving home a few hours later, without a single penny left over. Naturally, I was furious! I asked him how he had managed to spend so much money in a couple of hours on sweets and crisps. Soren looked shocked, and said, 'Dad, I spent it on all the other kids.' This excuse wasn't going to cut it with me, because I felt he had been given clear instructions, and I knew his strategy of tugging on my heartstrings. So, I challenged him further, reminding him that the money wasn't for the other kids, to which he replied, 'But, Dad, you always say our stuff is not our stuff, our money is not our money – it's God's!'

This is the power (and risk!) of developing a family culture of generosity, of thinking differently about our resources.

When we behold the most generous being in the universe, when we believe that everything comes from him, that 'our money is not our money', then we reflex with generosity.

An Extravagant Gospel

We see the extravagance of God demonstrated through creation, as well as God's generosity towards his people throughout the Old Testament. But nothing comes close to revealing the generous heart of God as his gift of salvation. The gospel story is the greatest story of generosity ever told. Jesus is God's most generous gift. 'For God so loved the world that he gave his one and only Son, that whoever believes in him shall not perish but have eternal life' (John 3:16). God gave of himself. God gave to a broken, wayward, underserving humanity. God gave the costliest of gifts, his much-loved, only Son. God gave in a way that caused him to suffer and die, such was the price of our salvation. God gave in a way that ripples and echoes through every fibre and aspect of our being. The gift of Jesus opens the door to receive all other blessings. 'He who did not spare his own Son, but gave him up for us all – how will he not also, along with him, graciously give us all things?' (Romans 8:32).

When we receive this free gift of Christ, we receive joy and peace and healing and wholeness and freedom. We receive eternal life. We receive all things! What an incredible gift! Does it not thrill your heart and make you want to jump up and down and shout 'yippee' and join with the apostle Paul in declaring, 'Thanks be to God for his indescribable gift!' (2 Corinthians 9:15)?

You see, when we remind ourselves of this truth and make it our daily input, it starts to renew and transform our minds. A *metanoia* takes place.[8] As we behold our generous God, and see just how generous he has been to us, it changes how we view our time, talents and treasures. We no longer feel we need to hold onto them or protect them. It is such a subtle but significant change of thinking. When I give my time, talents and treasure to others, I'm not really giving *my* stuff. Rather, I'm passing on what God has given to me, much like my son passed on my resources to the other kids in his youth group. When this shift takes place, no one needs to tell us to be generous and to give; it becomes as natural as blinking. Thanksgiving wells up in our hearts like a fountain that overflows with generosity towards God, expressed through generosity to those he has created.

I believe this is what Jesus means when he says, 'But seek first his kingdom and his righteousness, and all these things will be given to you as well' (Matthew 6:33). This is how our generous God's upside-down kingdom works. As we seek him, his kingdom and the foretastes or appetisers of our eternal home, in the here and now, we reflex with a generosity which extends his kingdom. Jesus said,

> Do not be afraid, little flock, for your Father has been pleased to give you the kingdom. Sell your possessions and give to the poor. Provide purses for yourselves that will not wear out, a treasure in heaven that will never fail, where no thief comes near and no moth destroys.
>
> Luke 12:32

Look to your Father and his generosity towards you, and reflex with a fearless freedom to give to the poor. When we receive all we need from our generous God, we find that we naturally start to outwork all of those biblical imperatives to care for the orphan, the widow and the stranger in the land, through how we steward our resources.

This way of kingdom living frees us from the worry of how our physical needs will be met, from the worry of what we will, 'eat, drink or wear' because we know that as we seek first the king and his kingdom, all those things will be given to us as well.[9]

We know that this reflex behaviour looks like addressing the needs of the poor around us because Jesus, who knew the provision of his generous Father more than anyone, reflexed with a care and compassion that placed the poor and needy at the front and centre of his ministry. And he makes clear that this is a priority for us in the mandate he gives us to seek first his kingdom:

> For I was hungry and you gave me something to eat, I was thirsty and you gave me something to drink, I was a stranger and you invited me in, I needed clothes and you clothed me, I was ill and you looked after me, I was in prison and you came to visit me. … Truly I tell you, whatever you did for one of the least of these brothers and sisters of mine, you did for me.
>
> Matthew 25:35–36, 40

This is part of the *metanoia* that takes place – our minds being transformed and made more Christlike, so that we live out something that looks more like Jesus to the world around us. So, caring for those close to Jesus' heart – the poor, the marginalised, the hurting – applies to how we use our money, but it applies to far more than that. It applies to every aspect of our lives. Yes, it's important to pay attention to how we use our money; after all it can so easily become an idol. Stewarding our money well has to flow out of keeping our eyes fixed on Jesus, and it helps us to live under his Lordship. But because God's extravagant generosity towards us is expressed in far more ways than simply finances, we too need a far greater understanding and definition of generosity, one that relates to every aspect of the kingdom.

One really helpful way of thinking about this is through the lens of the Five Capitals.[10] The Five Capitals are like a framework, which help us to think about the various resources we have. When we see the variety of ways in which our extravagant God has invested into us, we can be aware of how we can reflex with that investment into others. The Five Capitals are *financial, intellectual, physical, relational* and *spiritual*. God's generosity abounds to us in all five of these areas, and God's desire is that we steward and invest that which has been given to us, as we build his kingdom through our money, our creativity and intellect, our physical time and energy, through the relationships we build and through the wisdom and power of the spiritual energy God gifts to us. It is also important to note that these capitals have varied levels of significance – our spiritual capital is the most significant; our financial capital is actually the least significant. If you sometimes feel that you have little to give financially, that's OK. Being generous with whatever we have is the key, and it's also encouraging to know that often the greatest blessings to others can come through means other than our finances.

So, what has God given you that you could use to be a blessing to others? Maybe you are blessed with good health (physical capital) and could give some time to helping someone with practical jobs around their house? Perhaps God has invested an intellectual resource in you. You might be a maths whizz, or an incredible chef. Perhaps you could share those skills by volunteering as a debt advice counsellor or tutoring a child who is struggling with their schoolwork. You could use your culinary skills to cook meals for a family with a new baby or help serve meals at a homeless shelter. We all know that loneliness is a huge problem in our society, so the gift of relationship, time and friendship can be a huge blessing to someone who is struggling. When our church in Liverpool saw a government report showing our local area had some of the highest rates of loneliness in the UK, we set up a befriending project, and it has blessed and enriched the lives of both recipient and volunteer. And of course, our spiritual capital is the most significant and can be a generous outpouring to others where nothing else can fill their need. It amazes me how many people who would not even profess to have a faith are visibly moved by the offer of prayer when they are facing a difficult situation.

If you ever find yourself struggling to identify and give thanks for God's generosity to you, maybe you could make a list of the blessings you have experienced across all Five Capitals? God's gracious cycle of blessing relates to every aspect of the kingdom and every aspect of our lives. Surely we can say that, 'Every good and perfect gift is from above, coming down from the Father of the heavenly lights, who does not change like shifting shadows' (James 1:17).

The generosity reflex is the opposite of a vicious cycle. I'm not sure what you would call the opposite of a vicious cycle, perhaps *a gracious cycle*. As we preach the gospel to ourselves, and consider the generosity of God in salvation and the blessing of what has already been done for us, we reflex with generosity towards God and towards others. But that is only the first stage in this reflex. Because as we reflex with generosity towards others, God reflexes with further, greater blessing upon us! It is an incredible cycle of blessing and giving. God's reflex response when he sees our generosity is to pour out more blessing! 'One person gives freely, yet gains even more; another withholds unduly, but comes to poverty. A generous person will prosper; whoever refreshes others will be refreshed' (Proverbs 11:24–25).

We can behold our extravagant God, and reflex with extravagant generosity towards others, knowing that as we do so, God too reflexes in pouring out more blessing upon us.

So, hear me. This chapter is not about tithing. It is not even really about giving money. This chapter is about the extravagant generosity of God made manifest throughout the Bible, from Genesis to Revelation. It is about the ongoing story of a generous God, who invites his people into an abundant, life-to-the-full relationship, because of the work on the cross. Feed on that story. Preach it to yourself every time you feel the imposter of fear whispering in your ear to hold onto what you have. Find ways of embedding that story into daily life, through little things, such as giving thanks before meals, because you see what is before you as his bounty towards you. Raise high your pay cheque because you know he is the One who provided it. Give your time to help a family who need relational support. Practise spotting his goodness and provision in everything, and remember 'Freely you have received; freely give' (Matthew 10:8).

May you too find yourself surprised by how generous you become.

QUESTIONS FOR DISCUSSION

1. What are your biggest obstacles to becoming more generous?

2. In what ways have you experienced the generosity of God in your life?

3. Who could you bless this day?

PART 3

KINGDOM
REFLEXES

8

THE VICTORY
REFLEX

As we rest in Christ's finished work on the cross,
we reflex with victory and breakthrough.

Depending on the sort of church tradition or culture you are from, the concept of spiritual warfare will either be high on your radar or possibly not feature on it at all. Certainly, the sorts of Charismatic, Pentecostal, Evangelical churches I've been part of would have a lot to say on the topic, albeit not always from the widest perspective. When I talk to other believers about the topic of spiritual warfare, the response is usually polarised between blissful ignorance and unhealthy obsession.

I don't know how you would define spiritual warfare, but for me it is quite simple. Spiritual warfare is *anything* that pushes back the kingdom of darkness and advances the kingdom of light. It is anything that brings heaven to earth. It is likely that in your arsenal of spiritual weaponry you have one or two weapons you always turn to. You feel attacked by the devil, so you stick on some worship music and sing along. That is a great weapon of war. Or you pray in tongues; again, an excellent weapon of war. But spiritual warfare is far broader than that. Whenever we bring heaven to earth, that is spiritual warfare. So, if you feed the hungry and house the homeless, that is an act of spiritual warfare; heaven's light is invading the darkness of that person's life. Adopting or fostering a child is an act of spiritual warfare; taking a child out of a chaotic and damaging environment and giving that child peace and stability is all about bringing heaven to earth. When someone in the staffroom is going on about how they could never forgive the boss for how they have been treated, and you pluck up the courage to say that you have to forgive, because of how God has forgiven you, that is an act of spiritual warfare. Proclaiming something of the gospel is spiritual warfare. These are as much acts of spiritual warfare as deliverance ministry or binding territorial spirits.

If you are a follower of Jesus, you are at war. You are in a battle. As C. S. Lewis said in *The Christian Reflections*, 'There is no neutral ground in the universe. Every square inch, every split second is claimed by God, and counterclaimed by Satan.'[1] As Elisha prayed for his servant, when they were surround by the armies of Aram, "'Open his eyes, LORD, so that he may see." Then the LORD opened the servant's eyes, and he looked and saw the hills full of horses and chariots of fire all round Elisha' (2 Kings 6:17). We need to allow God to open our eyes to see that we are in a spiritual war, but more importantly that we are surrounded by heaven's armies.

Watchman Nee, one of the founders of the Chinese underground church made a clear call for Christians to engage with the reality of this spiritual battle:

The need today is for a company of overcoming saints who know how to wage war for the release of those under the enemy's deception. The church of God shall be defeated if she lacks members who know how to walk by the spirit and how to fight therewith against the enemy. May God raise up such![2]

We are called to be, 'more than conquerors through him who loved us' (Romans 8:37). Hopefully you are becoming so familiar with the concept of the reflex that you can see it in this verse. Any breakthrough or victory in our lives is simply a reflex out of who Jesus is and what he has done for us, in love, on the cross. When we see it this way, we see that any victory we experience really is *his* victory. Truly, 'The battle belongs to the Lord.'[3]

If you are from a church tradition that teaches on the topic of spiritual warfare, then it is quite possible that you, like me, major on *how* we fight – the things we have to do to be victorious. Even as a young lad in Sunday school I can remember learning about the armour of God, from Ephesians 6, and being taught how to put on the helmet of salvation, how to wield the sword of the Spirit, which is the Word of God, and how to raise the shield of faith to extinguish the fiery arrows that the devil was shooting at me – all good stuff, all very important. But as with everything in this book, these techniques and things I *should do* are only really effective when they sit on the right foundation. You can do all the binding and loosing you want, you can shout in heavenly tongues, you can wave your Bible prophetically like a sword at the devil, but if these actions are not reflexing out of the right stimulus, the right sort of input, I would suggest they are largely ineffective. Victory is a reflex to resting in God and his completed work on the cross. Victory is a gospel reflex.

Covenant and Kingdom Warfare

One of my key verses for spiritual warfare is 2 Corinthians 6:7 which talks about having 'weapons of righteousness in the right hand and in the left'. Now, I can't prove this through Greek exegesis of the text, but for me, the weapons of the right hand speak of *kingdom* weapons and the left hand speak of *covenant* weapons. I mean think about it, for thousands of years, rabbis and Christian scholars have talked about the 'right hand of God', the *dextera Domini*. Whenever we think of the right hand of God, we think of his power, his might, his strength. We think of kingdom. 'Save us and help us with your right hand, that those you love may be delivered' (Psalm 60:5; 108:6). 'Show me the wonders of your great love, you who save by your right hand those who take refuge in you from their foes' (Psalm 17:7). When God withdraws his right hand from Israel, they suffer defeat, 'In fierce anger he has cut off every horn of Israel. He has withdrawn his right hand at the approach of the enemy. He has burned in Jacob like a flaming fire that consumes everything around it' (Lamentations 2:3).

The Bible also mentions God's *left* hand, far less frequently, but it is referenced. Song of Songs 2:6 and 8:3 says, 'His left arm is under my head'. Proverbs 3:16 speaks of wisdom personified, 'in her left hand are riches and honour'. So, perhaps it is a bit of a stretch, but, for me, the left-hand weapons speak of covenant, identity, relationship, intimacy. I believe the dual covenant-kingdom concept is an incredibly helpful lens through which to understand spiritual warfare. As mentioned earlier, it is likely that any teaching you have received on spiritual warfare majored on the things you need to *do* in order to be a victorious Christian; a kingdom perspective. But, as is always the case, it has to be *covenant* first. Powerful spiritual warfare is first and foremost about resting in our true identity in Christ. It is the behold-believe-behave reflex once again.

So spiritual warfare and living in victory must undoubtedly start with beholding. It starts with seeing Jesus for who he really is. Jesus is the Victorious One. When we preach the gospel to ourselves, we remind ourselves that the victory has already been won. Through the death and resurrection of Jesus, the most decisive of victories was established. Sin was defeated. Death was defeated. The devil and all his demonic hoards were defeated forever. They were rendered powerless. Colossians 2:15 says, '[Jesus] disarmed the powers and authorities, [and] he made a public spectacle of them, triumphing over them by the cross.' That great hymn of Philippians 2:9 reminds us that now Jesus has been given the 'name that is above every name'. And Ephesians 1:20–22 talks of the power the Holy Spirit exerted,

> when he raised Christ from the dead and seated him at his right hand in the heavenly realms, far above all rule and authority, power and dominion, and every name that is invoked, not only in the present age but also in the one to come. And God placed all things under his feet and appointed him to be head over everything for the church.

Jesus is victorious. It is not like *the devil is powerful, but praise God, Jesus is a bit more powerful.* It is not like comparing Marvel superheroes: *Well, Hulk is powerful, but Thor could technically defeat Hulk.* It is not like kids in the school playground debating 'Top Trumps style' who is the greatest footballer. There is nothing and no one who can even come close to Jesus. His power is infinite and unlimited, and his authority is over all, and forever. Jesus is seated in heavenly places. All things are under his feet. Jesus is the victorious one. *Behold* him.

When we behold Jesus for who he really is, seeing him seated in heavenly places, it impacts how we see ourselves. Ephesians 2 goes on to say that not only is Christ seated on high with all things under his feet, but we – you and I – are, seated with Christ in the heavenly realms.[4] That is mind blowing! We can only make sense of it if we understand that we are 'in Christ': we are hidden 'in Christ' and clothed with Christ. Not only is Christ in us, but we are *in him*. So, where he is, we are there also, in the spiritual realms. And he is seated on high. That is the power of our identity, found in him.

Jesus fully understood his identity. As he entered the battlefield of the Judaean Desert to face his enemy the devil, he entered this contest from a place of the Father's affirmation, from the place of rest. So, when the devil attacked Jesus at the identity level, '*If* you are the Son of God' (Matthew 4:3, 6, italics mine), Jesus confidently fought back using the Word of God. God's Word, the Bible, is such a powerful weapon of war. It is the 'sword of the Spirit' (Ephesians 6:17). What makes it such a powerful weapon? First, it shows us who God is, and second, it shows us who we are in the light of who God is. That is the dynamic at play in Jesus' use of Scripture to combat the attacks of his adversary, the devil.

When you behold Jesus for who he is, and when you believe you are who he says you are, then you become a serious threat to the powers of darkness. You begin to advance the kingdom without fear. It is a reflex, as natural as blinking when poked in the eye.

As we change what we believe about ourselves, and how we see or behold Jesus, our behaviour reflexes out of this. This is fighting from the place of *ascension*. In Song of Songs, we see how intimacy with the beloved results in being called up to the mountain tops, and from there to look down on the lions and leopards. This is spiritual warfare, walked out from a place of rest in a covenant relationship; the power of fighting from the high place.[5] Any military strategist will tell you that to gain the high ground is to gain the advantage. I have a whole bunch of friends who are ex-Air Force. They will tell you that modern warfare is won by those who rule the air. That is why radar, satellites and drones are such important elements of today's armed forces. So, we fight from the vantage point of being seated with Christ in heavenly places. All things are under *our* feet.[6]

And we fight from the place of being seated. It sounds so counter-intuitive, but this is how we fight. We fight from rest. Victory is a reflex to rest. This is the pattern we see right through the Scriptures:

'The LORD will fight for you; you need only to be still' (Exodus 14:14).

'Now then, stand still and see this great thing the LORD is about to do before your eyes!' (1 Samuel 12:16).

'Be still before the LORD, all mankind, because he has roused himself from his holy dwelling' (Zechariah 2:13).

'Whoever dwells in the shelter of the Most High will rest in the shadow of the Almighty. I will say of the LORD,

"He is my refuge and my fortress, my God, in whom I
trust"' (Psalm 91:1–2).

'This is what the Sovereign Lord, the Holy One of Israel,
says: "In repentance and rest is your salvation, in qui-
etness and trust is your strength"' (Isaiah 30:15).

Rest is a powerful, left-handed, covenantal weapon of war. As
we rest, dwell and are seated in him (that is the input, the stimulus), we reflex with victory. The Lord fights for us.

Now, rest is not doing nothing. As with all reflexes, there
is effort required. It requires intentionality to rest in God.
When the world around you is shouting out, *Do something;
take matters into your own hands; it is down to you,* sometimes
the greatest single act of spiritual warfare is to say, *NO!* To say,
I am not cooperating. I am resting in God, my Deliverer. That is
an active process. In this sense, rest is an act of defiance.

Some of the greatest victories in history have come through
defiance, through non-cooperation. Think of Gandhi's peace-
ful protests in the 1930s. Thousands of lower-class Hindus
marched 240 miles to campaign against heavy taxes on salt,
and boycotted British goods. Or what about Rosa Parks? In
1950s America, she refused to give up her seat on a bus for
a white man. Warfare through defiance. Fighting through
stillness. Parents, you will know that kids are experts in this.
Victory through non-cooperation. Just being still. Resting in
God is one of the greatest acts of spiritual warfare you can engage in.

Rest is an act of confident defiance that tells the spiritual
principalities and powers that we have placed our trust in God.
And rest is active, because rest is surrender. As I have already
said, the effort of grace is surrender. So, rest is about yielding,

submitting to God. Again, this is a powerful act of spiritual warfare. 'Submit yourselves, then, to God. Resist the devil, and he will flee from you' (James 4:7). And in 1 Peter 5:6–9 we see the significance of resting and submitting to God as a work that aligns us for victory in the battle:

> Humble yourselves, therefore, under God's mighty hand, that he may lift you up in due time. Cast all your anxiety on him because he cares for you. Be alert and of sober mind. Your enemy the devil prowls around like a roaring lion looking for someone to devour. Resist him, standing firm in the faith, because you know that the family of believers throughout the world is undergoing the same kind of sufferings.

This is victory through resistance, through standing firm, through humility. Seven times in the New Testament, we are commanded to 'stand firm'.[7] It is a confident, defiant act of faith. And it reflexes with victory: the Lord fights for us.

Psalm 23 is most probably a familiar psalm to you. It is a beautiful and poetic picture of how our Good Shepherd leads us and guides us into a place of still waters and green pastures. One of the most powerful pieces of imagery in the psalm is in verse 5: 'You prepare a table before me in the presence of my enemies.' If I were to ask you to shut your eyes and picture that scene, what would it look like? As I reflect on that verse, I see a war scene and I see the enemies of God. But there in the thick of it all is a table. It is a table of choice food and drink, a celebratory meal. And around that table are a spiritual family. They are eating, they are drinking, they are laughing and celebrating. They are at rest. Around them the battle rages. But it's heaven's armies pushing back the desperately defeated powers of darkness while God's people are at rest. What an incredibly defiant picture of spiritual warfare.

Covenant identity, knowing who God is and who we are in him, is vital in spiritual warfare. As we rest in that, we reflex with victory and breakthrough.

Commissioned for Warfare

One important aspect of that identity is our commission. As followers of Jesus, we have been commissioned. When we think of commissioning, we perhaps think of a military or police officer. Commissioning is all about right identity reflexing with right activity. A commissioned officer acts with the full authority and backing of the one who commissioned him or her. They are empowered to do the things that they have been commanded to do. And likewise, we have been commissioned by Jesus to do the works of Jesus, to feed the hungry and refresh the thirsty, to welcome the stranger, to clothe those unable to provide for themselves, to care for the sick and imprisoned.[8] These activities are spiritual warfare because, according to our definition, spiritual warfare is anything that pushes back the kingdom of darkness and advances the kingdom of God. It is anything that brings heaven to earth. So, let us read our commission as disciples of Jesus with that in mind:

> He said to them, 'Go into all the world and preach the gospel to all creation. Whoever believes and is baptised will be saved, but whoever does not believe will be condemned. And these signs will accompany those who believe: in my name they will drive out demons;

they will speak in new tongues; they will pick up snakes with their hands; and when they drink deadly poison, it will not hurt them at all; they will place their hands on people who are ill, and they will get well.' After the Lord Jesus had spoken to them, he was taken up into heaven and he sat at the right hand of God. Then the disciples went out and preached everywhere, and the Lord worked with them and confirmed his word by the signs that accompanied it.

Mark 16:15–20

We have been given the authority to do the things that Jesus did. It is our commission. When I was a schoolteacher, my classroom overlooked a busy dual carriageway. It was a 30-mph zone, but this road was notorious for speeding motorists, which is not good when it's near a school. At least once a week, there would be a police officer at the side of the road with a speed gun. Now, a police officer is a commissioned officer, sent out with the full authority of the state. This particular police officer would walk out into the road, in front of the speeding car, and put his hand up. And the car would stop. Every time. The students I taught found it incredibly amusing, and would stare at the motorists as they got out of their car, making their walk of shame to the police officer who had pulled them over. Did that police officer have the physical force and power to stop a vehicle in and of himself? No. But because he was clothed in that uniform and had been commissioned with that authority, the driver stopped. The same is true of us. You and I have been commissioned to advance the kingdom. We have been clothed with King Jesus. We carry his authority and bear his name. As 2 Timothy 2:3–4 says, we are called to be a 'good soldier of

Christ Jesus', pleasing Christ our 'commanding officer'. That means you and I can stop the advancement of the kingdom of darkness and release the kingdom of heaven – right activity reflexing out of right identity; responsibility reflexing out of rest. When we really understand and believe who we are in Christ – as commissioned with Christ's authority, as ambassadors acting on Christ's behalf, as sons and daughters of the royal household – well, that radically changes how we engage with the world around us. We advance the kingdom without fear.

Behold Jesus the Victorious One, seated in heavenly places, with all things under his feet. *Believe* that you are seated with him. *Behave* by fighting from that place of victory and ascension, commissioned by your victorious Commander-in-Chief.

Worship as Warfare

It would be remiss of me to write about the reflex of victory through rest and not talk about worship. Worship, in whatever form it takes – whether that be congregational singing at a church service on a Sunday, or a sense of awe and wonder and appreciation as we climb a mountain or watch the sun rise – begins with *beholding.* As we behold God, we reflex with praise, thanksgiving and adoration. When the disciples saw the risen Jesus, their response was worship.[9] It was a reflex. Worship, as I've already said, is *focus.* And when we focus on Jesus, we reflex with faith. It is one thing to ask God for provision; it is another thing altogether to rest in Jehovah Jireh, the God who provides. As we behold him, faith rises in our hearts, and we align ourselves for breakthrough and victory.

We see this in the classic story of Jehoshaphat in 2 Chronicles 20. The people of God are outnumbered and surrounded by the Ammonites, the Moabites and the Meunites. King Jehoshaphat calls the people to take their eyes off their enemy armies and to fix them on God, 'We do not know what to do, but our eyes are on you' (verse 12). Jehoshaphat calls them to behold. To worship. You probably know the story, but if you don't, take a minute to read it. It is an incredible story of victory. As they send out the worshippers, God fights for them. The enemy is defeated. In other words, as they focus on God in worship, the reflex is victory. It is not an absence of effort. When you are in the thick of a battle – whether that be a fight for your health or your finances or your relationship – it takes incredible effort and resolve to focus on God in worship, to lift your eyes, and to rest in him. But only in doing so will we find breakthrough.

We see a similar dynamic in Acts 16. Paul and Silas have been thrown into a dark, intimidating prison because they had been preaching the gospel. They are chained up awaiting the sort of trial that could result in a physical beating or worse. And what are they doing? Acts 16:25–26 says,

> About midnight Paul and Silas were praying and singing hymns to God, and the other prisoners were listening to them. Suddenly there was such a violent earthquake that the foundations of the prison were shaken. At once all the prison doors flew open, and everyone's chains came loose.

It is such a simple principle. In that place of pain, Paul and Silas worshipped. They rested in God, and the reflex was victory. Sung worship is such a powerful way of preaching the gospel to ourselves. When I look at my morning devotional playlist, songs that I love to sing as worship at home each morning or in the car, they are songs totally about Jesus and his victorious death and resurrection. They are songs that call me to behold him. And as I do so, faith rises and I align myself for breakthrough. I remember the words of the psalmist, 'I keep my eyes always on the LORD. With him at my right hand, I shall not be shaken' (Psalm 16:8).

Follower of Jesus, we are at war. Jesus is victorious. Behold him. Keep your eyes fixed on him. See him seated in heavenly places, with all things under his feet. And believe that you are seated with him in that place of rest and victory. Our enemy, the devil, has already been defeated. So, fight from that place of victory and ascension. This is the behaviour that reflexes out of beholding and believing. Rest in God. Rest in that truth. Extend his kingdom from that place of resting in his finished work, and you will reflex with victory. The Lord will fight for you.

QUESTIONS FOR DISCUSSION

1. In times of conflict and challenge, what's your default response?

2. In what ways have you experienced God using you to push back the kingdom of darkness and advance the kingdom of light?

3. In what areas of life is God speaking to you about exercising more authority?

9

THE LEADERSHIP REFLEX

When we input into our identity as children of God,
we reflex with impactful kingdom leadership.

Whoever you are, whatever you are about in life … lead. The world needs leaders. The world needs the *right sorts* of leaders who will lead in the *right sort* of way. If you look at the many and varied problems in society, at home and abroad, we could rightly conclude that a lack of good leadership is at the heart of the problem, or at the very least a significant make-or-break part of the solution.

History is littered with good and bad leaders, or rather morally good and morally bad leaders, who have effectively influenced the world for better or worse. Consider and compare leaders such as Martin Luther King Jr, Mother Teresa or Nelson Mandela, who used their skills to effect positive change, with equally skilled leaders like Adolf Hitler and Pol Pot, who used their leadership skills to systematically persecute and annihilate whole people groups. Yes, these are extreme examples, but they illustrate the fact that leaders can exert their power either for the benefit or detriment of others. We need good or 'godly' leadership. Leadership, or an absence of it, will always make an impact. But distinctively Christian leadership creates a positive impact for eternity.

This chapter is a call to lead well. We need Christians, those in whom Christ dwells, to step up and lead in every sphere of society, be that in politics, healthcare, education, business and finance, arts and media, the family or the church. We need to be people of integrity who bring heaven to earth. As I mentioned earlier in this book, I truly believe that 'transformed people transform people'. And when you follow Jesus and seek to input all of his glorious gospel into your life, then you can't be anything but transformed.

The world needs your leadership.

Reluctant Leaders

As a church leader I spend a lot of my time trying to mobilise church members into areas of leadership. Raising up leaders is at the heart of distinctively Christian leadership. It is a challenging task, and I know from speaking to other church leaders that individuals are increasingly reluctant to take the lead. We are told by researchers that younger adults, especially women, don't want to lead.[1] And who could blame them? Look at the media and social media, and you will see that one of our favourite sports is to hunt and destroy those in power. The media regularly questions the leadership of female leaders by measuring them against stereotypes or being more focused on their appearance than their capability.[2] We love to cast stones at leaders for some misdemeanour they committed decades ago, but now we feel it disqualifies them from leadership. Accountability is important, but there seems to be so little grace, so little belief that a person has changed. Why would anyone want to lead?!

Others simply don't see themselves as leaders. They compare themselves with others in leadership roles and conclude that because they are not like this person or that person, or because they don't have the skills or experiences or title that others have, then they couldn't possibly be a leader. As a church leader looking to mobilise every man, woman and child in our church family into the mission of God, the range of excuses I have heard for why a person could not possibly lead is staggering: I'm too young. I'm too old. I'm a woman. I'm a pale male. I'm from an ethnic minority. I'm not educated enough. I'm too educated. I'm too sinful. And so on and so forth. They ignore the fact that the Bible is full of the most unlikely people who responded to God's call and stepped up to lead.

Take Abraham or Moses, for example, both of whom responded to God's call to lead in the later years of their life.[3] Moses responded to God's call to lead at the age of eighty.[4] He then went on to lead the entire nation for forty years until his death at 120. Both Abraham and Moses were deeply flawed characters, along with most of the other leaders of the Bible. Or what about Jeremiah or Gideon, who believed they were too young or too unimportant to step up and lead?[5] Timothy, who we know and celebrate as a young person is the only person in the New Testament to be described as a 'man of God' (1 Timothy 6:11). Or what about Deborah, a woman who led the entire nation of Israel?[6] Or Esther who used her influence and role to help God's people out of exile and slavery?[7] Or Junia, a woman described as 'outstanding among the apostles' (Romans 16:7). The apostle Paul was highly educated, but in contrast the apostles Peter and John were 'unschooled, ordinary men' (Acts 4:13). God specialises in using the most unlikely people to outwork his mission. The Bible is full of incredible, diverse leaders.

For some people, the biggest barrier to taking on leadership is their past experiences. They tried it, and it had a negative impact on their lives: those who took the promotion, only to be made the scapegoat when a project went wrong at work; those who found leadership required longer hours in the office, and caused strained relationships with their spouse and children, or led to excessive drinking that seemed to numb the pressure. There is a belief knocking around that leading others will ruin your life. It will chew you up and spit you out. It is a mindset we find in the church too: the idea that ministry leadership leads to burnout. And who could blame people for thinking this? It may well be their experience. Church history is littered with the burnt-out remains of past projects and kingdom leaders who found it all too much.

But leadership does not have to be like this. Burnout is a real danger when our kingdom activity does not reflex out of covenant identity. But when we reflex out of the stimulus of our true identity, as children of God, we find that kingdom leadership is also a light and easy yoke, just like the other reflexes we have already considered.

This is the covenant-kingdom reflex we have explored already. Jesus first calls us into intimacy, and then into activity. As we input the Great Commandment (love God and love others), we reflex with the Great Commission (go and make disciples). We are called to go into the world and lead. God's kingdom is advancing, heaven is coming on earth, and he calls his kingdom representatives to be part of ushering it in. This is what distinctively Christian leadership is all about.

A Different Kind of Leader

As followers of Jesus, I think it is OK to be a reluctant leader. It allows us to question our motivations, whether they be a need for control, personal gain, ego or something else. But more importantly, reluctance means that *when* we step into leadership, we do so with a sense of conviction and calling, that this is what God has purposed for us. When we know that, it plays a significant role in keeping us sustained in our leadership.

Leadership that endures and stands the test of time is a reflex. You can have a leadership *position*, a title, a role, a business card saying *CEO*, but effective leadership reflexes out of right identity. In other words, it's our *influence*, who we are. Once again, it is covenant then kingdom. Input the right stuff, and you will reflex with effective leadership.

Read any book on Christian leadership or listen to any Christian leader train on leadership, and undoubtedly they will define leadership as service. And rightly so. To lead is to serve. Jesus modelled this most effective and powerful leadership strategy in John 13 when he washed his disciples' feet. Perhaps I could encourage you to pause from reading this book and re-read this incredible passage, John 13:1–17. It will be well worth it!

What an outrageous, culturally inappropriate act of service … of leadership. In that moment, Jesus redefined leadership forever. And as we seek to live in the light of that, we find that whatever area of life we have been called to – whether that be crunching numbers in the boardroom, teaching Shakespeare in the classroom, or changing nappies in the nursery; whether we have a leadership title or role or not – we can all lead, because we can all serve. To be effective as leaders we need to put far more of our energies into getting our hands dirty and serving others than updating our social media profiles with 'inspiring' images of us leading.

But we can't *make* ourselves be servant leaders. Even with all the best intentions, *trying* to be a servant-hearted leader either won't work or will lead to burnout. That is because servant leadership has to start with right identity. Jesus took on the identity of a servant while paradoxically being the Son of God.[8] We too have the identity of a servant while also simultaneously being sons and daughters of God. This identity empowers us to service. If you take your sense of identity from your position of leadership or a title of leadership, then you can try to serve people as a sort of leadership strategy or technique, but it will be awkward, unnatural and unsustainable. A lifetime of joyful service reflexes out of a right identity as a servant. Martin Luther King Jr put it this way in his Drum Major Instinct speech in 1968:

> If you want to be important – wonderful. If you want to be recognized –wonderful. If you want to be great – wonderful. But recognize that he who is greatest among you shall be your servant. That is a new definition of greatness. ... it means that everybody can be great, because everybody can serve. You do not have to have a college degree to serve. You do not have to make your subject and your verb agree to serve. You

do not have to know about Plato and Aristotle to serve. You do not have to know Einstein's theory of relativity to serve. You do not have to know the second theory of thermodynamics in physics to serve. You only need a heart full of grace, a soul generated by love. And you can be that servant.[9]

All can lead, because all can serve.

We know that children imitate their parents. Babies only develop their speech by hearing, watching and copying the sounds that are around them. Young children love to join their parents and be involved with what they are doing, even if it is just a simple household task. As children of God, we know God as a Father whose desire is for his world, and that he delights in pouring out his grace and love. So, as our hearts are filled with grace and love, we find that we can't sit back and do nothing. We reflex with a passion to advance the kingdom, to bring heaven to earth. We are empowered to humbly serve the world around us, because we know we are both servants and sons and daughters of the royal household.

Two of my favourite words to describe the function of leadership are *influence* and *impact*. For me, they capture the essence of biblical leadership. They remind us that we can all lead because we can all influence others and we can all make an impact on the world around us. When you serve, you influence others. When you serve, you build relationship. Serving is a form of investment, much like parenting. We serve the needs of our children to equip and empower them to become the people God has called them to be and to take their place in society. Serving is far more than a transactional, 'I will do this for you so that you will do that for me'. Distinctively

Christian leadership is fuelled by love. Serving builds relationship. Serving builds loyalty. Serving increases the weight of your 'ask' of a person. It helps lift them from a dutiful response at the request of a leader to a joyful partnership in mutual service. We can all think of people who served and went the extra mile for us, and we know that when they ask something of us, we are there, we are in. One of the real joys of leadership is when we have served a person in such a way that they naturally start to serve others.

Serving increases leadership influence. And serving increases impact. This is because serving is fundamentally about meeting needs. This is why serving is kingdom activity. It brings the kingdom of heaven to earth, because as we serve we bring the provision and peace and presence of heaven to earth. A person's spiritual, emotional, physical and financial needs are met. The disciples had an immediate need prior to their Passover meal: they had dirty feet, a job that needed to be done, but no one had done it. So, the leader in the room stepped up and served.[10] Because that is what leaders do.

Once again, it makes me think of my elderly mother who at eighty-five years young heads into the city centre once or twice a week with a bag of food for the homeless. She does not see herself as a leader, far from it. But for me she models leadership in its purest form. Influence. Impact. Initiative. Service. Imagine the effect we would have if every follower of Jesus found their own version of that!

Leading from the Right Input

But what about the idea that leading will create burnout and ruin your life? The myth that leadership will have a negative impact on your life? Well, as with all myths, there is a kernel of truth at the heart of these myths; there *is* a cost to leadership, because there is a cost to serving. Leadership will place a cost on your time, your energy, your emotions and your finances. When I began teaching, I was rapidly given a series of promotions to roles that were beyond me. At the same time, I continued to lead within the church context, leading worship, leading small groups, leading a service/congregation. And by the way, did I mention that this was when we became parents of our first child? Looking back, I had got the input/outcome balance wrong. Ah, the value of hindsight! But through some very negative experiences of being totally overwhelmed, I began to learn the gospel stimulus. I began to develop priorities and rhythms for a healthier, more sustainable way of leading – and it's these I want to share with you now. I want to unpack three aspects of the gospel stimulus that cause us to reflex with healthy, sustainable leadership.

Leading as a Reflex to Intimacy

Leadership that endures and stands the test of time is leadership that reflexes out of intimacy with Jesus. This is the essence of distinctively *Christian* leadership. The gospel is primarily about intimacy, because the gospel is about restored relationship with God. Intimacy is about the depth and quality of that relationship. To say that good leadership must reflex out of intimacy sounds so simple, and yet I know it can be so difficult to live, not least because as we grow in leadership, we get busier, and therefore feel that we have less time. Something has to give. And if the *something* that gives is resting and abiding in God's presence (as it often is), then we are on a very dangerous trajectory indeed.

I've found that it is simply a lie from the pit of hell that I don't have time each day to spend with Jesus. In fact, I've found that I can't afford *not* to spend time with him. The gospel is the greatest input and stimulus for our lives. As I've said throughout this book, it's only when we abide in him that we bear fruit. All of our leadership *doing* is best viewed as fruit bearing. The sort of rootedness that leads to fruitfulness. So, abide and bear fruit.

In my devotional time, I come before God to remind myself of who he is and what he has done. It's a time where I gospel myself. I often think that a daily devotional time with Jesus works a bit like tithing. When I tithe, I'm demonstrating my belief that when I surrender the first 10 per cent of my income to God, the remaining 90 per cent becomes redeemed. The whole 100 per cent becomes incredibly fruitful. In the economy of the kingdom, 90 per cent surrendered goes far further than 100 per cent hoarded. In the same way, I've found that when I surrender the first part of my day to him – to worship and adore him, to rest in his presence, to listen to his voice through his Word, to claim and confess his promises – then the rest of my time becomes redeemed. It becomes far more fruitful. I have discovered that as I abide, I bear fruit. This is a discovery that saved my life when I was simultaneously a full-time schoolteacher, senior leader in a church and new parent. No one has time for a devotional time each day … until they learn the truth that we can't afford not to have that time.

The same is true on a larger scale of a day of rest: Sabbath. Sabbath was given to God's people in the Old Testament to facilitate and fuel relationship between God and humanity, to create space for humans not merely to rest, but to rest in

God ... to abide. Sabbath is all about relational intimacy. I discovered this on a visit to Israel, one Friday afternoon as the sun began to set. The start of a new day all starts at sundown on a Friday night. Everything shuts down – shops, taxis – in fact, there's a good chance if you are seen 'working', a devoted Zionist will throw stones at you.

God's pattern for life is one that starts with family time, rest, food and celebration. That is why if you look carefully in Genesis 1, the creation story, you will see it says, 'there was evening, and there was morning – the first day' (Genesis 1:5). God organised each new day to begin at sunset. Evening followed by morning. Rest followed by work. Covenant followed by kingdom. The evening speaks of family time, food, sleep. The morning speaks of activity. In the modern western world, we work, *then* rest. We rest *from* work. But in the Jewish world, they rest, *then* work. They work *from* rest. The pattern is reversed. It might not sound like much of a difference, but it will make all of the difference to your life and leadership. On a natural level, Sabbath fuels human relationships. On a deeper level, it fuels relationship with our Creator. It is an essential stimulus for healthy leadership: rest reflexing with work.

In Exodus 33 we meet Joshua, the young assistant to the leader Moses. Moses was preparing Joshua for leadership succession and transition, and Moses centred his time with Joshua around the Tent of Meeting, a place of intimacy with God. I have learnt more about leadership through regular times of prayer and worship with my mentors than through any leadership programme. In verse 11 it says that, 'Moses would return to the camp, but his young assistant Joshua son of Nun did not leave the tent'. Joshua was hungry for more of God. This is what qualified him to lead. If you are looking to step up to lead a project, ministry or take on a new position, I would suggest the number one quality to personally develop is intimacy.

We know that this was true of King David, a man after God's own heart. In one of his psalms, David writes that, 'Then the righteous will gather about me because of your goodness to me' (Psalm 142:7). There is something about God's favour, his blessing, his goodness, on us that draws people to follow us. A reflex. Likewise, in Psalm 110:3 we read, 'Your troops will be willing on your day of battle.' I like how this is translated in the New King James Version, which says, 'Your people *shall* be volunteers in the day of Your power; In the beauties of holiness, from the womb of the morning, You have the dew of Your youth.' Church leaders often debate how to increase volunteering. My answer would be that *volunteering is a reflex to the presence of God*!

In the world of leadership, there is a culture of boasting about how many hours you work. It is endemic among church leaders. We are all *so* busy. Maybe it stems from the Protestant work ethic and human nature to try to please God. After all, it is important to work hard and work, 'as working for the Lord' (Colossians 3:23). Or maybe our boasting is rooted in an identity issue. We want recognition and affirmation for all the effort we are putting in. Perhaps we believe that our work is only important, that *we* are only important, if we are rushing around relentlessly, wearing the bags under our eyes as a badge of honour for all that kingdom work we are doing. What if we put our efforts in their proper place under Jesus' Lordship? What if we remembered that it is the King who is advancing his kingdom, and he calls us to bear fruit, only by abiding in him? What if we exercised our faith in a way where we *do* less and rest in him more? Maybe we would get less done. But the promise of Jesus is that as we abide, we bear fruit. If you want to lead well and live well, if you want to lead and thrive, then make intimacy with Jesus your number one priority and goal.

Leading as a Reflex to Love

Healthy leadership that endures and stands the test of time, is leadership that reflexes out of love. Love is like rocket fuel for leaders. And love is at the heart of the gospel. But what does it look like to lead as a reflex to love?

To lead as a reflex to love means that we have to be daily receiving God's love *for us*. This is very much a continuation of the point I have just made about the stimulus of intimacy. We have to daily get under the fountain of God's love for us.[11] It is possible that right now, you feel weary in your service and leadership. If that is true of you, then know that the Father loves you with all of his love, all of the time. Make it your highest priority to find ways of receiving that love. He wants to lead you beside still waters and into green pastures; he wants to restore your soul.[12] You may need to unbusy yourself and build more effective relational rhythms into your life in order to experience that. Effective leadership always requires us to lead ourselves well first. Actively and intentionally adding the right inputs into our lives so that we reflex with the right outcome could be considered self-leadership. It is about personally experiencing the reflexes we have been exploring throughout this book so that we can lead others into them; giving out from what we have received. And God wants to fill you with his love until it flows out expressed as love for others.

Leadership is also about reflexing out of a deep love and compassion for others. If you have led for any period of time, you will know that you can't lead, or at least you can't lead effectively, if you have lost your love for the people you are called to lead. You will also know how incredibly easy it is to lose love for people, because people can be difficult! At these times it is important to *behold*, to look to God. As we gaze upon him, we are reminded that his patient leadership of us, his people, flows out of his deep love and compassion for us. He knows our frame, our weaknesses; he knows that we are dust. He knows that the heart of a person is desperately wicked above all things.[13] At times, in the Old Testament, God comes close to giving up on his people. And yet his covenant faithfulness compels him to continue to love his creation.[14]

When we look at the life of Jesus, we see his healing ministry was intensely demanding. Everyone wanted a piece of him, a touch, a word, a miracle. But he also set boundaries that allowed him to lead from intimacy with the Father. Jesus often withdrew with the Father to be filled with his love.[15] As we explored in the chapter on the love reflex, Jesus' ministry reflexed out of love and compassion for those he led. He saw that they were like sheep without a shepherd. When he saw their suffering and brokenness, his love reflexed with action.[16] Ultimately his love for you led him to the cross; the ultimate act of service, of influence, of impact, of leadership.

God's leadership of you reflexes out of his love for you.

And our leadership of others, if it is to be healthy and impactful, has to reflex out of a love and compassion for those we lead. Think about the person or people who make leading difficult for you. God loves them with all of his love, all of the time. When he sees them, he sees and understands their brokenness and need. So, ask God to fill your heart again and again with love for those you lead. It is what qualifies us to lead, and it is what sustains us to lead.

Leading as a reflex to love also comes from *what* we love. Healthy leadership is a reflex to our God-given passions. That means figuring out how to align our work, our service, our leadership with the things that make us come alive. As the old adage goes, 'Do what you love, and you'll never work a day in your life.' It takes time to discern what it is that we love, and it's important to do this with the guidance and help of others. When you are young, just starting out, the best leadership advice I can give you is just to serve, have a go, do whatever. But as we mature in our leadership and in our walk with the Lord, we find that approach is not really sustainable. We start to discover more of who God has uniquely made us to be, and we find greater ease as we align our leadership with that. Our leadership becomes more natural. But it takes effort, time, thought, intention and planning to align your leadership with your God-shaped personhood.

In the classic 1981 film *Chariots of Fire*, Eric Liddell is faced with a decision. Based on a true story, Eric, an Olympic-medal-winning runner, international rugby player, and Christian missionary, has to decide if he is going to become a full-time Christian minister or if he is going to pursue a career in sport. And this is what he says, 'Wherever we go we either bring people nearer to Christ or we repel them from Christ. I believe God made me for a purpose, but he also made me fast! And when I run I feel his pleasure.'[17]

I often joke that when I run, all I feel is a tight pain across my chest! It is not natural for me. I was not made for speed. But I think what Eric was saying was that when we lead or serve out of the wrong motivation, ultimately we will repel people from Christ. But when we lead in a way that is full of Jesus' life and joy, it is deeply attractive. It is a powerful witness. So, let your leadership and service be an expression of godly pleasure. That's what Eric Liddell did. He used his athletic ability to extend God's kingdom and lead people to Jesus.

If we are to lead in a healthy and sustainable way, we have to lead out of our God-given passions. He's made each of us uniquely, in his image, for a specific purpose. This is far more than filling rotas and delegating tasks in order to be productive.

I'm aware that it may not always be possible to change your job or your tasks so that you're doing more of what you love and less of what you don't love. I get that. I have experienced it myself. But we *can* change the *way* we do the things we have to do.[18] I first learnt this as a student on a summer job. Boy, have I done some mind-numbing temporary work as a student. I remember working in a margarine factory in a heatwave. It felt like there was grease everywhere! But I made it my ambition to be the most productive worker on the factory floor. I also made sure I entertained the other workers through a series of pranks, all too devious to mention in this book. But we had a laugh. And I soon got promoted to the lard line, and then the office. Whatever we do, we can do it with great love. We can be the person who brings life and fun and cake into the workplace. We can transform our surroundings into a place that people love to be. And that is leadership. Lead with love.

Leading as a Reflex to Grace

The final leadership reflex, and perhaps the most important, is this: healthy, enduring leadership reflexes out of grace. It is a gospel reflex. When we input the gospel of grace, we reflex with a different kind of leadership. It is what makes our leadership distinctively Christian. Of course, all that we do as Christians is only healthy and good to the extent that it reflexes out of God's grace in our lives. This is the singular point of this book. So, it ought not to surprise us that this is true of our leadership. But to what extent is it true of your leadership?

In one sense, I am talking about *saving grace*. Our leadership should be distinctive because of our relationship with Jesus. Because of God's grace, you have passed from death to life. The same power that raised Christ from the dead is now at work in you. If that doesn't impact your leadership, nothing will. But I am also talking about leadership that reflexes not only out of *saving* grace, but also out of *sanctifying* grace, the grace of God available to you in each and every moment of the day; grace that is new for you each morning to transform, empower and equip you in your leadership.

This is how the apostle Paul led. Paul's leadership was a reflex to the grace he received. And his leadership was remarkably impactful. Think about the incredible churches Paul planted. Think about the numerous and fruitful leaders Paul raised up. Think about the significant hardship and suffering Paul endured as a leader. And yet for Paul, it was all a reflex to grace. In 1 Corinthians 15:10, he says these words, 'By the grace of God I am what I am, and his grace to me was not without effect. No, I worked harder than all of them – yet not I, but the grace of God that was with me.'

Paul's leadership reflexed out of the grace God had given him. Of course, that is what grace means, isn't it? It means *what is gifted to us*. Paul led out of what he had received. And herein lies the secret to sustainable leadership. Lead out of what you have received, out of what you are receiving. As Jesus said, 'Freely you have received; freely give' (Matthew 10:8). Leadership is a reflex to grace.

We see the same idea in Philippians 2:13, 'for it is God who works in you to will and to act in order to fulfil his good purpose'. God is at work in you. What is his work in you? He works to transform your will so that you act in a way that out-works his will. The desires in you are God-given. That desire to end homelessness or to foster a child or provide outstanding education for disadvantaged kids, that is like God poking you in the eye. It is God at work *in us* so he can work *through* us. It is a reflex.

Leadership burnout happens when we help people beyond what we have grace for. Leadership weariness happens when we lead things we have not been gifted for.

For Those Who Lead Within the Church

A final word on leadership within the church (but everyone else can and should listen in).

Who would have thought how difficult leadership could be in a church? Not me! It shocked and continues to shock me. So, it is important that you receive grace. That you allow God's grace to abound in you. You are doing an incredible job. I pray that when you go to bed on a Sunday evening, having preached your heart out, all you will hear is the affirmation of the Father who delights in you, his child. I pray that every time you serve in Sunday school, you will know just how much it delights the heart of God.

On reflection, some of the greatest stress I've experienced in church leadership has come from trying to lead the church like a business. It is not. We can learn from business, and good

practice can help us become good stewards of the precious resources entrusted to us. But I would encourage you to explore
with your leadership team what it means to be distinctively
gospel in your leadership. At Frontline Church, we do measure stuff. We set goals. We have a strategic plan with Key
Performance Indicators. I think we do all of that sort of stuff
pretty well. But it is not what is going to lead us into life and
health and impact as a church.

Neither can we take someone else's story and strategy and
make it our own. I would encourage you to read this book
in the same way I read every Christian book: with a healthy
degree of curiosity, listening to what the Holy Spirit is speaking to you for your own journey and context. Often, Christian
books are written by leaders who are reflecting retrospectively,
towards the end of their journey. God has powerfully worked
through them over the years, but they set off on that journey
without much of a clue. So, when it comes to church or ministry strategy, I would encourage you to come up with your own
untested hypothesis, your own God-inspired vision that may
or may not work. The point is, fruitful leadership is a reflex
to hearing and obeying what the Spirit is saying to *you*. By all
means, learn from others and be inspired by them, but write
your own story.

Occasionally you will meet a remarkable Christian leader,
someone God has used mightily. Over time, they might have
developed all sorts of strategies and techniques and resources.
But if you dig into their story, you will almost certainly find
that their fruitfulness began, and continued, with intimacy.
Someone who reflexes with great kingdom leadership does
so because they have inputted the stimulus of their covenant
identity. They intimately know their heavenly Father. They

know their place as a child of the King. They have received his love and grace, which reflexes in their passion for Jesus. And they can't help but have a love for those around them.

Input the covenant identity that brings intimacy, love and grace, and you will reflex with healthy, sustainable, impactful kingdom leadership. The world around us will be transformed.

QUESTIONS FOR DISCUSSION

1. How distinctively Christian or 'gospel' is your leadership?

2. Can you think of a time when you really had an impact on a person or group? Why was that?

3. What are some of the ways in which you could input intimacy, love and grace from God, to sustain your leadership?

10

THE GOOD
NEWS REFLEX

*As we input the stimulus of the good news, we reflex
with proclamation and demonstration that God's
kingdom is available and attractive to all.*

If ever there was something that made me feel a failure as a
young Christian it was evangelism. I knew I should tell people
about Jesus, but the thought terrified me. I believed the gospel
was *good* news – not just good news but the *best* news![1] Not
even just the best news for me, but the best news the whole
world needed to hear. How could I keep it to myself? In fact, the
weight of this was so heavy on me that I would frequently walk
in the town centre, aware that many of those around me would
spend an eternity in hell without Jesus. But rather than this
spurring me to share my faith, it simply paralysed me and left
me feeling rubbish. Fear, by the way, is a terrible stimulus. When
fear pokes you in the eye, the reflex action is usually unhelpful!

So, I used to set myself evangelism targets in an attempt to be a 'proper' Christian. At the age of seventeen, I would go into the city centre and not leave until I had told at least one person about Jesus. I would sit on the bench in the shopping centre, wait for someone to sit next to me, and then try to start a conversation with them. I had every reason to believe that this would be an effective form of evangelism. After all, I had watched my grandmother sit on the same bench every Saturday from as early as I could remember right up to her death.[2] Mum would take my brother and me shopping, and we would return to the bench only to find someone sat next to my gran in tears as they gave their life to Jesus. It was a fairly regular occurrence.

So, there I was each week, sat on the bench, my knees shaking, my palms sweating, hoping for someone non-intimidating to sit next to me … an easy win. I was completely focused on getting the right outcome. Making the grade. What I hadn't realised was that, for my gran, her witness was a reflex to the stimulus of a life lived in devotion and intimacy with Jesus. For her, sharing her faith was as natural as blinking.

What's the Big Deal?

At the beginning of our journey together in this book, I asked you to consider if your gospel was big enough. I suggested that perhaps your version of the gospel was so reduced, so small, that it only related to a salvation transaction on day one of your Christian walk. Yes, the good news invites us into that walk. It shows us that Jesus died for us, for our sins, so that we can have a relationship with a holy God. Amen to that. But the good news of Jesus is far more expansive than that. As we've seen, our personal application of the gospel stimulus impacts and transforms every single aspect of our lives as followers of Jesus. It is good news that reflexes with joy and generosity and victory, to name but a few outcomes. But it seems to me that not only can our gospel be too small for *us*, it can also be too small for others. The gospel we often share can be too insignificant to really capture the attention and imagination of those around us who don't yet have a relationship with Jesus.

You may have experienced that Monday morning workplace scenario where a colleague is raving about a film or TV series that was just so amazing, the best thing ever, and you find yourself simply nodding politely, 'oohing' in the right places, and saying you will watch it … without the slightest intention of doing so. Why? It simply didn't capture your attention or appeal to you in a way that stirred you to do something about it. It didn't resonate with you, perhaps because it didn't sound that enjoyable, or you couldn't see how it would enhance your life.

Honestly, as much as it saddens me to say so, I have seen the same look in the eyes of people with whom I've tried to share the gospel. My words simply didn't capture their imagination or stir them to action. It didn't resonate with who they are. I suspect that is true for many who hear the gospel. So often, the gospel we share lacks breadth and depth and colour and texture, it fails to fill the senses and capture the imagination.

So, what exactly is the *good news*? Or what makes the good news *good*? That might sound like an odd question to ask. *The good news that Jesus' death gives us life* is the central theme of this book. But I wonder how those around us, those who don't know Jesus, would answer that question? It might need to be reframed for them. For example, we might ask, 'What is it that you are really longing for in life?' Or 'What is it that you desire deeply that you do not have, that if you had would make all the difference?' Instinctively, we know that humanity longs for deep, lasting relationships. You only have to look to the latest film releases, series on Netflix or top-selling fiction to see that the world is longing for something more than the here and now. We know that people long to be free from past experiences and from the shame that holds them back from being who they desire to be. People are longing for contentment. Fulfilment. Meaning and purpose. They long for connection to something bigger than themselves and the world around them, even if they don't know how to articulate it. The reason the gospel is such good news for all people is that it reveals how all those human needs can be met fully, in a way that nothing else can.

Now, if you were to have asked the first Jewish followers of Jesus what good news was for them, their response may well have included something about freedom from the burden of the law. The good news was an invitation into grace, to live under the light and easy tallit-yoke of Jesus. That would have been incredibly attractive to those first hearers of the good news.

As the apostle Paul began to bring good news to the Gentiles (the non-Jew), a different aspect or facet of that same good news emerged. It was the message that Greeks and Romans could be free from the empty pursuit of pleasure and free from gods that controlled every aspect of their lives. Again, this message resonated deeply with those hearers.

Different perceived needs, same gospel. Same solution to the need.

N. T. Wright, in his book *Simply Christian*, describes these various, in-built needs within humans as *the echoes of a voice*.

We express them (the voice), and as we do so, something of the answer echoes back to us. Our needs give us a momentary glimpse into a new, better world. As humans, we have inherent needs for justice, beauty, meaningful relationships and for connection to something bigger than us, bigger than the world around us. Like an echo, God uses these needs to call back to us.

And so, for us, as followers of Jesus, reflexing with good news looks like following Jesus in such a way that responds back to this world. The world calls out with a longing for justice, and we, as God's people, respond with *this is what real justice looks like*. The world calls out for real relationship, and the church echoes back with the sound of true community and family. Our words and works demonstrate how a person's deepest needs and desires can be met in Jesus.

This way of viewing the good news is far more powerful than a reduced gospel that merely focuses on securing a place in heaven when you die. It is an invitation into a transformed life here on earth, here and now. It is an invitation into the rebuilding of society, of bringing heaven to earth – transformative work that reflexes out of a transformed life. As Jesus said, 'I have come that they may have life, and have it to the full' (John 10:10).

So, what does that look like? As we input the stimulus of a bigger gospel, a gospel that makes a tangible difference in every aspect of our lives right now, today, it ought not to surprise us that we find we reflex with sharing the gospel in much more natural, expansive, and varied ways. That has certainly been my experience. As I have learned to input the good news, the thought of sharing good news no longer fills me with dread. In fact, I am not sure I give much thought to it at all now. It has become a natural reflex.

A key verse that reflects the importance of this reflex is found in the prayer of the psalmist in Psalm 51: 'Restore to me the joy of your salvation and grant me a willing spirit, to sustain me. Then I will teach rebels your ways, so that the lost will turn back to you' (my paraphrase of verses 12 and 13).

There is so much in this psalm about how the input of good news reflexes with the outcome of sharing good news. The key reflex point here is the word *then* in verse 13. 'Restore to me the joy of your salvation and grant me a willing spirit, to sustain me. *Then* ...' As we gospel ourselves, reminding ourselves of how we have been cleansed and forgiven, salvation-joy is restored to us. Joy starts to bubble up within us. As we have already explored, joy is the natural reflex to the gospel stimulus. But the experience of the psalmist is this: as salvation-joy is restored, *then* he finds that he teaches the lost God's wonderful ways and calls them to turn back to God, to repent. The psalmist's witness reflexed out of his encounter and experience.

When Milena[3] first came through the doors of our church, it was into the food bank. She had fled an abusive relationship in Poland and was in desperate practical need. As part of our food bank outreach, we offer prayer and relational support, and so one of the volunteers did just that. Milena was drawn into relationship, into community; it was compelling and attractive to her. Like an echo or a dream, humans instinctively know we are created for community, but it was not until Milena experienced *true* community that the gospel started to make sense to her. She began to volunteer at the food bank too, a transformed life reflexing with transforming the world around her. Through her work with the homeless in the city, she began to connect with other Polish speakers, and so a Polish church plant emerged.

It seems to me that when Milena heard God calling her into relationship, she instinctively knew the owner of this voice,[4] because she had experienced the sort of unconditionally loving relationships and community that only God could provide. The gospel was fleshed out and modelled – the good news of Jesus was expressed to Milena in a way that met a need. Like the discovery of a hidden spring of water that quenches a thirst,[5] it felt like good news.

We might think of all of our reflexes working towards this point. As we input the good news into our lives, we reflex with joy and generosity and love. These outcomes are observable to others. Like the blink of the eye or the swing of the knee, they evidence and reveal something that is going on in us, at a hidden level. The world calls out with longing for these things, and hears and *sees* them in us as God's people.

Communities of Good News

Milena's story is typical of those who come to faith in our church community – whether that be through a food bank, or one of our homeless houses, or students who end up sharing a house with a Christian flatmate. They gradually experience a new kind of community, a community different to any group, team or family they have ever been part of before. In a time and place where families are fragmented, and community is eroded, this aspect of the good news that says 'you can belong' is good news indeed.

If you were to enter our church building throughout the week, perhaps to access one of our community projects, there is a good chance you would be greeted by one of our staff members, a giant of a man called Max.[6] When Max encountered

Jesus, it was through a colleague at work called Dave.[7] Both Max and Dave were car salesmen with a history of drug addiction. Dave had encountered Jesus some time before and had told Max that Jesus could turn his life around too. Dave was the embodiment of good news to Max. In Dave, Max saw something that he desired. Max began to attend one of our communities and found the sort of friendship, acceptance and accountability he had longed for. In some ways, this was not a new kind of community for Max. He had experienced a similar type of community as a child, when he was part of a Sunday school. So, for Max, it was like *coming home* – it was both new and familiar. And it's through community that Max has grown in God's grace. His life has been transformed in multiple ways.

It is in community that the gospel is most powerfully fleshed out, modelled and echoed back to a person. A community that loves unconditionally empowers those who join the community to love in such a way. A community that models deep satisfaction and joy in Jesus is a community that empowers those who step into it to leave behind all those other things that they turned to for satisfaction. Yes, we flesh out the gospel to the world as individuals, but together, in community, we incarnate the good news in ways that are far more varied and impactful.

A More Authentic Way of Sharing Good News

When we think about *being* good news or embodying good news, it's also helpful to think in terms of how we can share good news as an authentic and unique expression of who God has made us to be.

When both our sons were born, we couldn't stop telling people about them. It was such a life-changing, joyous moment, that we wanted everyone to know about it. We sent a text message to everyone in our phone contacts. We posted photos to our elderly relatives. We made numerous boast-posts on social media. It was all we talked about!

You see, when something is good news, and we really know it's good news, we tend to share that with other people. Evangelism is a natural reflex to receiving good news. If you have watched the best TV series ever, you want to tell people about it. If you have eaten at a new restaurant and it was amazing, you want to spread the word. You *become* an evangelist for the show or restaurant. Sharing good news is a natural, instinctive reflex to receiving good news. But we all do that differently. For some of us, we shout it from the rooftops to anyone who will listen. Others of us will share with those who are closest to us around a meal table. Some of us will talk less and simply invite people to participate and share with us somehow in our good news. The point is that good news is worth sharing, but we all share it in different ways.

In Ephesians 4, we read of five different types of leadership gifts given to the church: the apostle, prophet, evangelist, shepherd (pastor) and teacher.[8] Evangelists are just one of the five, so not all of us are evangelists by gifting, as I discovered when I tried to replicate my gran's evangelism methods on a supermarket bench. For her, that was natural, authentic behaviour that reflexed both out of her deep intimacy with Jesus, but also out of her natural gifting as an evangelist. So, though we are not all gifted to be evangelists, we are all called to be witnesses of the good news we have experienced and to share that good news with others.[9] And allowing our *witness* to reflex out of our *gifting* is a powerful and effective way of sharing good news.

Not long ago, one of our missional communities organised a car-free high street day, along with other local resident groups.[10] Various stalls were set up. There was food, music, bunting. The atmosphere was fantastic, and loads of local residents were hanging around, chatting and getting to know one another.

In the planning stage, the missional community gathered to think about what gifts and skills they had that they could draw on to reach out to the people they would meet. One person, a schoolteacher called Steve,[11] decided that his best contribution would be to dress up as a Russian oligarch and set up nine chessboards side by side and challenge local residents to simultaneously compete with him at chess! As you can imagine, it drew quite a crowd, and opened up lots of good, relationship-building conversations. Alongside this, a couple of the more prophetically gifted community members set up a gazebo tent with a sign offering prayer and a blessing. Throughout the day, there was a steady stream of people who entered the tent and received prayer. The team would also share with each individual what they felt God had placed on their hearts for that person. For many, this was moving and uplifting; it echoed back to them that innate human desire to be connected into something bigger, often described in our contemporary culture as *spirituality*.

When a *community* of believers with various giftings all play their part together it can have a powerful impact. For Steve, his contribution came naturally to him. He had great fun (and won all the games, by the way). When something is authentic and fun, it's a good indicator that it's a reflex. We don't all need to be chess-playing Russian oligarchs. But we do each need to find our own expression that helps us build relationships with those who don't yet know Jesus. Steve went on to invite a number of people onto an Alpha course. For someone whose fivefold ministry gifting is a teacher, Alpha provides a great way to share the gospel because the course delves into what the Bible says about the good news.

Remember the story about Milena at the food bank? Well, the woman who befriended Milena might not be considered an evangelist. But she used her pastoral gifting, expressed through her love and care, to naturally lead Milena into the kingdom. In all these stories, we see good news reflexing out of who God has made people to be: the embodiment of good news.

Spirit-Empowered Good News

Though it's important that we share good news as a reflex of who we are uniquely made to be, it is also important to know that it is not all down to us. Early on in this book, I talked about the tension between *grace* and *works* and how the reflex principle involves learning to input God so that we no longer strive for the right *results*. There is something much more natural about sharing the good news when we know that God is the one advancing his kingdom. When we remember that our responsibility is to put God in his rightful place, to behold him and to worship him, then our proclamation and demonstration of the gospel becomes a reflex, rather than something we feel we must *achieve*. Whereas we might want to do our best to be obedient to him and seek first his kingdom, it is *God* that is at work in people's hearts. It's only by his power that we can share the good news. And it's only by his power that any of us ever respond to the gospel. Some people will reject the good news when we share it with them. Knowing it's not all about our effort helps us to entrust those individuals to God rather than taking undue responsibility for their decision.

In his life and witness, Jesus modelled a life empowered by the Holy Spirit and full of the Father's love, as he sought to usher in his Father's kingdom and bring God glory. When Jesus saw the crowds in Matthew 9:36, he was filled with the love of the Father as he saw the needs of those around him 'harassed and helpless'. But his compassion didn't just remain a feeling. It resulted in action. He called his disciples to the harvest, telling them, 'The harvest is plentiful but the workers are few' (Matthew 9:37). His heart of love led him to respond and to call his disciples to join with him.

For Jesus, this spirit-empowered action happened through *words*, *works* and *wonders*. With his *words*, Jesus proclaimed the good news, whether to fishermen, Pharisees or those on the fringes of society. In the same way, in the stories I shared earlier, people came to faith in Jesus because they had heard the gospel, perhaps by receiving a prophetic word, having a friend explain the good news, or learning through an Alpha course what it means to put their faith in Jesus. The Christians in those stories were moved by God's love and led by the Holy Spirit to share his good news to the people around them.

Jesus' compassion also led him to model the good news through his *works*. Just think about how Jesus interacted with sinful tax collectors, or defended the woman caught in adultery, or made time for children.[12] The way he lived demonstrated the good news in action. Similarly, as followers of Jesus, we can embody this good news, particularly when we come together and demonstrate the good news as a community. In the examples I shared earlier, individuals experienced the love and welcome of a family, as Christians demonstrated the Father's love to them, whether through a food bank, a new family or a Russian oligarch!

And Jesus also demonstrated the future hope of heaven through his miracles – through *wonders*. Jesus healed the sick, multiplied food and wine, stilled storms, walked on water and drove out demons. I believe a crucial aspect of our witness is the demonstration of gospel words through gospel wonders. And I believe each believer today can reflex with miraculous power and gifts of healings. After all, this was the early church's experience. As we see this played out through the book of Acts, we see miraculous signs and wonders accompanying those who believed. That might sound well and truly outside of your experience or comfort zone, but if we see the miraculous as a natural reflex outcome to the stimulus of the Holy Spirit's work in our lives, then it takes the pressure off. It's not about us; it's about what the Spirit might want to do through us.[13]

When one of our young-adult missional communities were asked to think about how they could share good news in the build-up to Christmas, they reflected on how many in their community were musical, and decided to host an open-mic night. Lots of the young adults performed, and they invited some of their non-Christian musical friends to perform too. About halfway through, a short gospel message was shared, and people were invited to discuss the message around tables. During the discussion, one of our student workers felt the Holy Spirit prompt him to ask the guy in front of him if he had ever had a shoulder injury. And so he did. He took the risk.

The guy looked shocked. An old sporting injury to the shoulder had recently flared up, causing him considerable pain. So, they prayed for him, there and then, and God turned up and healed the guy's shoulder. I would love to tell you that he then gave his life to Jesus, but he didn't. However, he is on a journey. And he is connected into community. God is at work in his life and, on that particular night, God certainly got his attention.

Ongoing Repentance

When Jesus first started talking about the good news, he accompanied it with a call to repent: 'The kingdom of God has come near. Repent and believe the good news!' (Mark 1:15). His words, works and wonders were about inviting people into a different way of living. We might find the word *repentance* a bit jarring in today's society, but repentance is an essential first step in understanding and accepting the gospel. As I shared with you in chapter two, repentance is so much more than saying 'sorry' to God. Repentance means *to change one's mind*, which is the literal translation of the Greek word *metanoia*. It's choosing to turn away from the things that are only imitations and that cannot truly satisfy, and to look fully at the true God who we were made by and for. We finally discover the true voice behind the echoes we hear in our world.

When we first receive Jesus, it is because repentance has occurred. In other words, we have recognised that our previous outlook was wrong. Perhaps we might have viewed ourselves as the boss of our own life, or maybe we saw ourselves as a basically decent human who had no need for God. When we repent, we turn away from those mindsets, and instead we align our thinking, our *transformed* thinking, with

God's Word. We know that true repentance, a true change of thinking (believing) has taken place because we start to reflex with new and changed behaviour.

Repentance is a key part of our initial acceptance of the gospel, but it is also to be practised throughout the entirety of our Christian lives, as an ongoing gospel stimulus. Repentance need not be a heavy, sackcloth and ashes, weeping and wailing type of thing. As I have learnt to input the stimulus of the gospel into my life, I have discovered repentance to be a joyful, life-giving process. It allows me to throw off any shame, guilt or condemnation that I have allowed to rest heavy on my shoulders, and to step into greater intimacy with Jesus. And, as we have seen in Psalm 51, a repentant heart receives the joy of salvation and naturally reflexes by inviting others into that better way of thinking and being.

For me, one of the key areas of ongoing repentance is around self-effort, of trying to do things in my own strength and ability. Self-effort is fundamentally opposed to the gospel because it is contrary to grace. Grace is all about God giving to me freely and underserved; God empowering me in my weakness and inability to do the things he has called me to do, such as sharing his good news with others. So, the gospel stimulus of ongoing repentance helps me to draw on that power and equipping in all areas of life, especially in my witness, because repentance brings me back to my own brokenness and need of a Saviour. It means that when I share and embody the good news, I am not calling others to be like me, because I am amazing or somehow better than them. That is a sure-fire way of putting people off the good news. Rather, I am somehow communicating through my words and works that I have a great need, and Jesus has and continues to meet that need. And he can do the same for them too.

So, ongoing repentance helps me to walk in intimacy with Jesus; to recapture salvation-joy; and to keep grace front and centre in all I do – all of which empower and equip me in sharing good news.

Ongoing Revelation

In Revelation 2:1–7, the believers who made up the church in Ephesus were praised for their deeds, their hard work and their perseverance. And yet, they had lost the one thing that mattered. They had lost their first love. Oh, from what heights they had fallen!

When we lose our first love – and believe me when I say that this is always the case – the light on our lampstand diminishes:

> Yet I hold this against you: you have forsaken the love you had at first. Consider how far you have fallen! Repent and do the things you did at first. If you do not repent, I will come to you and remove your lampstand from its place.
>
> Revelation 2:4–5

There is something about our love for Jesus that relates to the lamp on our lampstands. What do the light and lampstand symbolise? I think they represent the good news in our lives. And if we don't truly love Jesus and his good news, then we don't let our light truly shine. As Jesus said in Matthew 5:14–15, 'A town built on a hill cannot be hidden. Neither do people light a lamp and put it under a bowl. Instead they put it on its stand, and it gives light to everyone in the house.'

Our lampstand is our witness – we share the gospel in a dark world. We are responsible for maintaining and cultivating first love in much the same way the priests were commanded to keep the fire on the altar burning.[14] When we lose our first love, we lose the stimulus that reflexes naturally with witness. We no longer really shine forth Jesus to those around us. But when we cultivate our first love, our hearts are filled with salvation-joy, and the gospel leaks out of us. We reflex with holiness, love, joy and generosity, which not only causes those around us to ask questions about the way we live our lives, but also means others can experience God's love and generosity through us.

So how do we regain and maintain our first love? We input the stimulus of the gospel. In prayer, we confess as David did in Psalm 18:28 that, 'You, LORD, keep my lamp burning'. It is about who he is and what he has done. It is about the gospel. As we preach the gospel to ourselves, as we explore new facets and nuances of the matchless story, joy is restored to us, and we reflex with sharing Jesus, our Source of Joy, with others.

The more we tell ourselves the gospel story, and the more we engage with the gospel daily through ongoing repentance and revelation – the more wonderful and thrilling it becomes. Our gospel gets bigger. We become more fluent in sharing the gospel with others, because we have become more fluent in preaching it to ourselves. Salvation-joy is restored to us. First love is stirred up. And we reflex in ways that lead people into relationship with Jesus.

QUESTIONS FOR DISCUSSION

1. Does sharing the good news come naturally to you, or do you feel like your stimulus for evangelism is fear (or another negative stimulus)?

2. How do you share good news with people in the unique way that God has made you?

3. What might it look like to share good news through the community of believers that you belong to?

EPILOGUE

SOLI DEO GLORIA

I wonder if I were to ask you to sum up your life – who you are and who you aspire to be, and what your life is all about – what word or few words you would use? What words might be emblazoned in ink across your chest or chiselled in your gravestone?

Throughout this book, I have said that if I had to find a phrase that captured the essence of the stimulus input, it would simply be *the gospel*. The good news of who Jesus is and what Jesus has done for us is *the* ultimate stimulus. Find ways to input that truth more and more into your life, day by day, and you will be both transformed and transform the world around you.

But what is the essence of that transformation? What is the word, or words, that capture *the* reflex, *the* goal, *the* desired outcome? What one thing, more than anything else, are we trying to achieve?

Growing up, those within my church tradition continuously emphasised the *glory of God*. The sermons they preached and the weightiness of the language they used all focused on God's glory. Every prayer ended with those words in various forms, 'And we will give you all the glory. Amen.' Likewise, having travelled through parts of India and met many wonderful, godly Christians, you can be sure that when you pay them a compliment, you are unlikely to get a 'Thank you' as a response, but rather a 'Glory to God, brother'. I use those examples only with the utmost respect. Those Christians have sought to be very careful that God alone receives all the glory and that humans take no credit for what God has done. And to varying extents, we see this throughout the evangelical and reformed churches. It would seem that their ultimate goal is the glory of God.

Soli Deo gloria.

Undoubtedly, the articulation of this goal stems from the Reformation, which happened over five hundred years ago with the likes of Luther and Calvin – radicals who called the church to strip away its theatrics, pomp and ceremony and sought to promote and celebrate only One. *Soli Deo gloria*, to God alone be the glory; this was the heartbeat and heart cry of the Reformation.

It is a truth that became enshrined in the Westminster Shorter Catechism of 1647, which reminds us that the chief end of man is to 'glorify God, and to enjoy him forever'.

But what precisely does it look like to glorify God? How do we make that phrase more than a mantra or a big ending to a great prayer? How do we live it out, flesh it out? What is our part in truly glorifying God?

I can find no better way of answering those questions than this; as you and I become more like Jesus, God is glorified. The people of God transformed into the likeness of God is the key to glorifying God. And so, if I had to land the reflex outcome as one thing, it would be that we become more like Jesus, that we are transformed more and more into the image of Jesus. And this indeed is the reflex outcome that takes place as we input the stimulus of the gospel. As we daily preach the good news to our souls, we reflex with holiness; we become more like the Holy One. We reflex with love, generosity and joy; in other words, with Christlikeness.[1] We reflex with victory, with servant leadership, with witness. We become more like Jesus our Lion-Lamb, our Servant-King. All the outcomes we have considered throughout this book are encapsulated in this one idea: input the stimulus of the gospel, and reflex with a life that increasingly looks like him.

But the reflex goes further. As we are increasingly transformed, God is increasingly glorified. And God's big goal, his desired outcome is that, 'the earth will be filled with the knowledge of the glory of the LORD as the waters cover the sea' (Habakkuk 2:14). God's big purpose is that the earth will become filled with and aware of his glory. How does this earth become filled with glory? The earth, or rather the peoples of the earth, become more and more aware of the glory of God as they encounter you and me, his glory bearers. There is something about you and me that reveals to the world who God is.

So, the world needs you to look increasingly like Jesus. No, that is not an excuse to wear a bed sheet, hippie sandals and to stop shaving. Becoming more like Jesus looks like becoming more of the person God uniquely created you to be, or to paraphrase the words of Dallas Willard, you become who Jesus would be if he were you.[2] Or, to use the words of Søren Kierkegaard, 'With God's help I will become myself.'[3] The world needs you to be the you God had in mind when he knit you together in your mother's womb. It is a call to be transformed. Glorified. This is what it means to give God the glory.

Glorified through the *outcome* and glorified through the *process*.

Gospelling Others

God is supremely concerned with his glory filling the earth. That means that everything we've reflected on throughout this book cannot simply be about us as an individual. The reflex principle has to be more than how we personally reflect more of God's glory as we reflex in response to the gospel. To push the medical reflex metaphor a little further, not only are we the patient, but, we are also called to be like the doctor who shines the light into the eye of another, or who taps the knee of someone else to stimulate response. It's about gospelling ourselves *and* gospelling others. Indeed, the very act of inputting the gospel will lead us to reflex with gospelling those around us.

We see this in the life of Tudor housewife Anne Askew. Anne lived in the sixteenth century and was a wealthy, educated mother of two, a Protestant convert married to a Catholic landowner. Anne lived in a unique moment in history: the Bible had recently become available in English but was strictly regulated. As decreed by Henry VIII, the king at the time, this radical book was only to be read in private, in the home, by educated men.

With her newly found faith, Anne Askew defied the king by reading the gospels aloud in public. She, like many others, became colloquially known as a *gospeller*. Anne took it upon herself to proclaim the good news to large crowds outside Lincoln Cathedral. It wasn't enough for Anne to have a personal revelation of the gospel; she wanted to share that with others. For Anne, this began her journey towards the Tower of London, where she was eventually burned at the stake. As the only women ever to be tortured in the tower (her diary makes for a fascinating read), Anne was unique. But many other gospellers also risked and lost their lives for the proclamation of good news. You see, for Anne and the other gospellers, the gospel stimulus had such an impact on their lives, that they were prepared to die for it.[4]

Anne Askew is perhaps an extreme example. You and I are unlikely to be burned at the stake. But the point is this: though reflexing is the *natural* way to live the Christian life, it doesn't mean it's the *easy* way to live the Christian life. It may be costly. Though we may gain friends, we may lose others. We may be called to sacrifice hopes and dreams for the bigger vision of God's kingdom, sustained and empowered by God's grace. And though we input the gospel, we may not always see the outcome. Anne Askew's life was cut short, but no doubt the impact of her life continued to reflex for many years beyond her death. You see, a biological reflex is instantaneous. You hit the knee, and it immediately reflexes. But our spiritual reflexes are different. We may input something that takes years before we see any outcome. That's the way of the kingdom, the reality that we live in the *now* of God's kingdom but also the *not yet* of God's kingdom. We see some transformation now, both in terms of our own lives, and also in terms of the transformation experienced by those we input into … but there are other things we may never see this side of heaven.

Jesus commissioned his followers to go and make disciples, but he also told them, 'Whoever wants to be my disciple must deny themselves and take up their cross daily and follow me' (Luke 9:23). We are called to give of ourselves in pursuit of seeing the transforming work of the gospel, in our own lives and in the lives of those around us. When we do that, it might not always look like success – the outcomes might not seem to tick the boxes – but we know that we give honour and glory to Jesus by following in his ways.

All Glory to Jesus

Let me finish this book by asking you a question. As you reflect on your process of inward transformation over the years, who deserves the credit? Who gets the glory? As you have developed and grown as a person, who gets the praise? Likewise, when we think about the transformation of those we have invested in over the years, who is to be applauded? You see, if Christianity is nothing more than a self-help program, a self-improvement technique, then the glory for any growth or positive change or achievement will be rightly yours. Well done. You worked hard and lost the weight, learnt a language, overcame your fears. You grew that ministry or led that project really well. Or well done for being good and not naughty. Pat yourself on the back. Treat yourself, you deserve it. If you put the work in, you deserve the credit.

But the process of becoming more like Jesus is nothing like a self-help programme. It is a reflex. It is the outcome to the right sort of stimulus. And when we understand that transformation is an eye-blink, knee-jerk reflex to what God has done for us, then we realise that we can take no more credit for our growth than we can take credit for breathing or blinking. We have simply found ways of positioning ourselves to experience the transformative work of the Holy Spirit.

Neither can we take any credit for the development of those we have the privilege of welcoming into the kingdom, or those whom we disciple. Being an effective disciple-maker simply looks like being a gospeller of others – finding ways of poking those around us in the eye with good news! I feel immensely humbled to have had such people in my life, people who have called me to lift my eyes off myself and behold Jesus. They have gospelled me. And in the process, I have been transformed.

A process as natural as blinking.

I would humbly suggest that viewing our process of spiritual formation as a *reflex* enables us to glorify God. As we develop habits of daily inputting the gospel, as we learn how to apply the stimulus of the completed work of Christ – the *outcome* glorifies God; we more fully reflect the glory of God to the world in which we live. And the *process* glorifies God – the wonderful working of the Spirit can be seen in our lives.

Truly, all the glory belongs to him.

Thank you, Jesus.

And we all, who with unveiled faces reflect the Lord's glory, are being transformed into his image with ever-increasing glory, which comes from the Lord, who is the Spirit.

2 Corinthians 3:18

ACKNOWLEDGEMENTS

Special thanks to the Frontline Church family who have lived out so many of the principles of the book.

My senior leadership team: thanks for your encouragement and support throughout this whole process, especially during a global pandemic.

Steve Lightfoot, for your pedantic attention to detail.

John Sloan, for your deep medical insights.

Greg Schofield, for being the first person to encourage me to capture these thoughts in a book.

Huge thanks to 100 Movements Publishing for your support and contributions to the book.

And thanks to my family, and especially Joan, my mum, one of the real stars of this book who has modelled the true essence of the gospel to me all my life.

NOTES

Introduction: The Problem

[1] Denis Campbell, 'UK has experienced "explosion" in anxiety since 2008, study finds', *The Guardian*, 14 September 2020, https://www.theguardian.com/society/2020/sep/14/uk-has-experienced-explosion-in-anxiety-since-2008-study-finds.

[2] Sarah Young, 'Eco-Anxiety: Children are Losing Sleep and Having Bad Dreams Over Climate Change, Study Finds', *The Independent*, 3 March 2020, https://www.independent.co.uk/life-style/children-climate-change-sleep-nightmares-eco-anxiety-greta-thunberg-a9371191.html.

[3] Otherwise known as FOMO (Fear of Missing Out).

[4] Matthew 9:20–22; Mark 5:25–34; Luke 8:43–48.

[5] Mark 5:41.

[6] Malachi 4:2 NKJV.

[7] See Rob Bell, *Velvet Elvis* (Michigan: Zondervan, 2005), 47.

1 The Reflex

[1] See John 7:37.

[2] Psalm 23:5.

[3] See, for example, in Matthew 13:24–30; 13:31–32; 13:33; 13:44–46.

[4] Rich Lusk, 'The Metaphor is the Message: Thomas Aquinas on Biblical Interpretation and Metaphor', (University of Texas, 2000), https://www.trinity-pres.net/essays/metaphor-is-message_aquinas.pdf.

[5] For example, see Romans 11:6.

[6] Charles Spurgeon, *The Metropolitan Tabernacle Pulpit Sermons*, Vol. XV (London: Passmore & Alabaster, 1869), 146.

186 | REFLEX

2 The Stimulus

1 Used by permission, the4points.com.

2 See 1 Corinthians 1:18–31.

3 Tom Wright, *Paul for Everyone: Romans Part I* (London: SPCK, 2004), Glossary.

4 Jerry Bridges, *The Discipline of Grace* (Colorado: NavPress in alliance with Tyndale House Publishers, 1994), 51.

5 August Nebe, *Luther as Spiritual Adviser* (Lutheran Publication Society, 1894), 207.

6 See Ephesians 2:8–9.

7 John 6:29.

8 Bridges, *The Discipline of Grace*, 51.

9 Dallas Willard, 'Live Life to the Full', https://dwillard.org/articles/live-life-to-the-full.

10 Dallas Willard, 'The Human Body and Spiritual Growth', https://dwillard.org/articles/human-body-and-spiritual-growth-the.

11 Luma Simms, *Gospel Amnesia: Forgetting the Goodness of the News* (California: CreateSpace Independent Publishing Platform, 2013).

12 Fred Sanders, *The Deep Things of God: How the Trinity Changes Everything* (Illinois: Crossway, 2010), 106.

3 The Covenant-Kingdom Reflex

1 Mike Breen, *Covenant and Kingdom: The DNA of the Bible* (3DM International, 2011).

2 Here are seven short kingdom parables told by Jesus: Matthew 13:31–32; 13:33; 13:44; 13:45–46; 13:47–50; 13:52; Mark 4:26–29.

3 See Leviticus 9:22–24.

4 See 1 Samuel 16.

5 See Isaiah 6:1–8.

6 See Acts 2:42–47; 16:5.

7 You can read more about our friends' story in Esther Addley, 'Making up with the Joneses: how Covid-19 has brought neighbours

closer', *The Guardian*, 5 June 2020, https://www.theguardian.com/
world/2020/jun/05/neighbourliness-to-the-fore-its-been-the-high-
light-of-our-lockdown.

[8]   1 Peter 4:11.

[9]   Matthew 12:34.

4 The Holiness Reflex

[1]   Ben Sternke unpacks this really well in his blog on grace and effort,
'You Can't Do It Alone, But It Will Not Be Done For You', 9 February
2015, https://bensternke.com/grace-and-effort/.

[2]   Luke 4:12.

[3]   Malachi 3:10.

[4]   Paul often addresses his letters to 'saints', for example Romans 1:7
NKJV.

[5]   Isaiah 61:10.

[6]   Interview with John Piper, 'What is God's Glory?' *Desiring God*,
22 July 2014, https://www.desiringgod.org/interviews/what-is-gods-
glory-2.

[7]   See Exodus chapters 33–34.

[8]   1 Peter 1:16.

[9]   This process of deification or *theosis* is only complete upon our seeing Jesus face to face. See 1 John 3:2 and 2 Peter 1:4.

[10] Genesis 1:27.

[11] Genesis 13:12.

[12] 2 Samuel 11–12.

[13] The Ten Commandments begin with this idea, to have no other gods
or to make no idols. Exodus 20:1–4.

[14] Mary Oliver, *Upstream: Selected Essays* (New York: Penguin: 2016), 11.

[15] In Amos chapters 1 and 2, Amos lists all the sinful nations that surround Israel. In Amos 3 to 6, Amos calls out Israel for being no
different.

[16] David Foster Wallace, 'This is Water by David Foster Wallace', *Farnam*

Street, April 2012, https://fs.blog/2012/04/david-foster-wallace-this-iswater/.

5 The Love Reflex

1 Writing this in 2020 in the midst of the Covid-19 pandemic makes this story feel even more uncomfortable. The ways we can express love to others have categorically changed during this time. My mum, being Mum, of course continued to find ways to express this kind of extravagant love to the homeless and spent time during the lockdown months in the UK handing out sausage rolls on the streets, while wearing a facemask!

2 His name has been changed.

3 John 13:23–25; 19:26–27.

4 Richard Foster, *Streams of Living Water: Celebrating the Great Traditions of Christian Faith* (London: Hachette UK, 2017), 56.

5 Names changed. You can read more of their story in Sarah McDermott, 'Our foster child asked us to adopt him – by drawing himself on to a family photo', BBC News, 19 September 2020, https://www.bbc.com/news/stories-54071599.

6 John 3:16.

7 Lamentations 3:22–23.

8 Marva Barnett, *To Love Is to Act: Les Misérables and Victor Hugo's Vision for Leading Lives of Conscience* (Chicago: Swan Isle Press, 2020).

9 Romans 5:8.

10 See Matthew 14:14; 20:34; Luke 7:12–15; John 11:38.

11 Joseph Fletcher, *Situation Ethics: The New Morality* (Louisville: Westminster John Knox Press, 1966), 87.

12 For a fuller account read Nehemiah 1:4; 2:17–18.

13 Nehemiah 3.

14 Nehemiah 6:9.

6 The Joy Reflex

1 C. S. Lewis, *Mere Christianity* (New York: MacMillan, 1960), 120.

2 C. S. Lewis, *Letters to Malcolm: Chiefly on Prayer* (San Diego: Harvest, 1964), 93.

3 See 2 Corinthians 1:22; Ephesians 1:13–14.

4 Helena Bolhuis, *Broken Beauty: Reflections of a Soul Refined by Cancer* (Oregon: Wipf and Stock Publishers, 2020), 104.

5 See Hebrews 10:25, for example.

6 I wholeheartedly believe it is important to care for oneself, as an expression of the love for oneself that empowers us to love our neighbour. For a provoking article on the limitations of the self-care movement and how the gospel can empower self-care practices, see Marshall Segal, 'The Insanity of Self-Care', *Desiring God*, 14 March 2016, https://www.desiringgod.org/articles/the-insanity-of-self-care.

7 The word *beatitude* comes from two Latin words *beati sunt*, meaning *blessed are*.

8 Her name has been changed.

9 John 11:35.

10 John 11:33.

11 Isaiah 53:3 NKJV.

12 Hebrews 12:2.

13 Douglas Todd, 'Meet the creator of the "Laughing Jesus" (photo)', *Vancouver Sun*, 19 January 2014, https://vancouversun.com/news/staff-blogs/meet-the-creator-of-the-laughing-jesus-photo.

14 Isaiah 61:1.

15 1 Timothy 1:11 talks about 'the gospel concerning the glory of the blessed God'.

16 C. S. Lewis, *The Weight of Glory* (San Francisco: Harper One, 2001), 26.

7 The Generosity Reflex

[1] Timothy Keller, *The Prodigal God: Recovering the Heart of the Christian Faith* (London: Hodder & Stoughton, 2009).

[2] Leviticus 19:9 and 23:22 are examples of how landowners and farmers were to leave the edges of the fields to be harvested by the poor in the land.

[3] See Matthew 11. We looked at this in the previous chapter.

[4] Sources: https://www.royensoc.co.uk/facts-and-figures; https://tinyurl.com/y6tv29my; https://www.newscientist.com/article/mg22730301-400-the-nature-of-crops-why-do-we-eat-so-few-of-the-edible-plants/.

[5] C. S. Lewis, *Mere Christianity*, 192.

[6] 1 Chronicles 29:2.

[7] 1 Samuel 13:14; Acts 13:22.

[8] See chapter two for further exploration of *metanoia*. *Metanoia* is the Greek word for repentance, and literally means *to think in a new way*.

[9] Matthew 6:25–34.

[10] For more information on the Five Capitals see https://blog.fivecapitals.net/five-capitals-what-why.

8 The Victory Reflex

[1] C. S. Lewis, *Christian Reflections* (Michigan: Eerdmans, 1978), 33.

[2] Watchman Nee, *The Spiritual Man*, Vol. 3. (New York: Christian Fellowship Publishers, 1977), 280.

[3] My paraphrase, from 2 Chronicles 20:15 and 1 Samuel 17:47.

[4] Ephesians 2:6.

[5] See Song of Songs 4:8; 6:4; 6:10.

[6] See Romans 16:20.

[7] Mark 13:13; Luke 21:19; 1 Corinthians 15:58; 1 Corinthians 16:13; 2 Corinthians 1:24; Galatians 5:1; Ephesians 6:14.

[8] Matthew 25:31–46.

[9] Matthew 28:17.

9 The Leadership Reflex

[1] Denise Restauri, 'Why Millennial Women Do Not Want to Lead', *Forbes*, 16 July 2012, https://www.forbes.com/sites/deniserestauri/2012/07/16/why-millennial-women-do-not-want-to-lead/?sh=1f11cadf2b7a cites the pressures to be perfect and the fear of being judged. See also Kim Arellano, '4/7 – The Generational Shift in the Workplace: Are WE Ready?', *Integral Leadership Review*, Learner Papers, April–June 2015, http://integralleadershipreview.com/12937-47-the-generational-shift-in-the-workplace-are-we-ready/ which cites the rejection of hierarchical structures as a factor in this.

[2] Susan Devaney, '5 Times Politicians Faced Unfair Criticism Over Their Appearance', *Vogue*, 6 February 2020, https://www.vogue.co.uk/fashion/gallery/female-politicians-appearance-clothes-criticism?image=5e3c33b9b20c8e00095011ce.

[3] Genesis 12:4.

[4] Exodus 7:7.

[5] Jeremiah 1:7; Judges 6:15.

[6] Judges 4:4.

[7] Esther 4:15–16.

[8] Philippians 2:5–11.

[9] For both the text and audio of the full sermon see Martin Luther King Jr, '"The Drum Major Instinct", Sermon Delivered at Ebenezer Baptist Church', (Stanford University, 4 February 1968), https://kinginstitute.stanford.edu/king-papers/documents/drum-major-instinct-sermon-delivered-ebenezer-baptist-church.

[10] John 13:1–17.

[11] Romans 5:5.

[12] Psalm 23.

[13] Jeremiah 17:9.

[14] For example, 2 Kings 13:23.

[15] Luke 5:16.

[16] Matthew 9:36.

[17] Hugh Hudson, director, *Chariots of Fire* (Allied Stars Ltd: 1981).

¹⁸ We might not always be able to align *what* we do with our God-given gifts, but we can align *how* we do it. For example if God has given you a teaching gift, then whatever your job, develop and train others. If God has gifted you pastorally, care for those around you. For further reading on this I highly recommend Alan Hirsch's book *5Q: Reactivating the Original Intelligence and Capacity of the Body of Christ* (Atlanta: 100 Movements, 2017).

10 The Good News Reflex

1 The word *gospel* simply means *good news.*

2 Nell was the lady from the local church who took my mum in when she left home, and I grew up relating to her as my grandmother.

3 Her name has been changed.

4 See N. T. Wright, *Simply Christian: Why Christianity Makes Sense* (London: SPCK, 2006), 38.

5 See Wright, *Simply Christian*, 20.

6 His name has been changed.

7 His name has been changed.

8 Ephesians 4:11–16. These five types of leadership gifts are often referred to as the fivefold ministries. An apostle, meaning *sent one*, would be someone who extends the gospel, looking to pioneer and plant new expressions of God's kingdom. A prophet refers to someone who looks to know God's will and share it with others. An evangelist is someone who has an infectious passion for sharing the gospel with non-believers. A teacher is someone who has insight and revelation to share from God's Word. A shepherd (or pastor) is someone who cares for the needs of others and demonstrates God's caring heart. For more information on this have a look at www.5Qcentral.com.

9 The Great Commission, Mark 16:15.

10 A missional community is a group of Christians who have a shared vision to demonstrate and proclaim the good news of Jesus to a particular place or people group. They look to connect with, and create

space for, those outside of the church wanting to explore faith. It is usually part of a larger church congregation.

11 His name has been changed.

12 Luke 5:27–31; John 8:1–11; Mark 10:13–16.

13 If you want to grow more in this, see John Wimber and Kevin Springer, *Power Evangelism* (Michigan: Chosen Books, 2009).

14 Leviticus 6:12–13.

Epilogue: Soli Deo Gloria

1 As I said at the start of the book, bearing fruit is a biblical metaphor for a reflex. As we abide (that's the input), we bear fruit (that's the outcome). As such, we could add all the fruit of the Spirit here as examples of how we reflex with Christlikeness. We reflex with the love, joy, peace, forbearance, kindness, goodness, faithfulness, gentleness and self-control that is perfectly seen in the person of Jesus (Galatians 5:22–23).

2 Dallas Willard, 'How Does the Disciple Live?' https://dwillard.org/articles/how-does-the-disciple-live.

3 Søren Kierkegaard, *Papers and Journals* (London: Penguin, 1996), 295.

4 See Bettany Hughes, *Forbidden Families: Anne Askew*, BBC Radio 4, Episode 2, 18 August 2009, https://www.bbc.co.uk/programmes/b00cxr1k.

DUNDEE'S TRAMS
AND BUSES

WALTER BURT

AMBERLEY

First published 2014

Amberley Publishing
The Hill, Stroud
Gloucestershire, GL5 4EP

www.amberley-books.com

Copyright © Walter Burt, 2014

The right of Walter Burt to be identified as the
Author of this work has been asserted in accordance
with the Copyrights, Designs and Patents Act 1988.

ISBN 978 1 4456 3461 6 (print)
ISBN 978 1 4456 3472 2 (ebook)

British Library Cataloguing in Publication Data.
A catalogue record for this book is available from
the British Library.

Typeset in 9.5pt on 12pt Celeste.
Typesetting by Amberley Publishing.
Printed in the UK.

Introduction

The aim of this book is to allow us to have a little wander back through time to, say, a period just before the introduction of Dundee's first tramcars in 1877. The Victorian era saw great advances being made in all walks of life, and transportation was certainly at the forefront at this time. Electric power, and the invention and gradual development of the internal combustion engine, ushered in a new era. Dundee was one of the areas to embrace these new ideas and technologies with open arms.

This book is by no means an comprehensive look at either the trams or buses of Dundee, but merely a look at some of the various vehicles to have trundled, rattled or rolled along the streets of this great city of jam, jute and journalism. There are more in-depth publications out there, some unfortunately no longer in print, which do the specified subjects more justice than I possibly could within these pages.

I would like to think that the images I have used, from a great many sources, show not just a view of any particular tram or bus, but also the ways in which Dundee itself has changed through the last century and a half. Perhaps a street or building that no longer exists, or a particular vehicle or location: there is bound to be something of interest in these pages, not just for the transport enthusiast, but for the local amateur historian out there like myself.

A Brief History

Dundee & District Tramway Company Limited

The first horse-drawn tram route was opened by the Dundee & District Tramway Company in August 1877 with a gauge of 4 feet 8.5 inches, and operated from the post office to Dalhousie Terrace. Within a couple of years, new lines were being opened to Lochee and to West Park Road. These were closely followed by lines to Morgan Hospital and Baxter Park. On 20 June 1885 the first regular steam tram operation to Lochee began, but it wouldn't be until 1894 that further extensions opened to Fairmuir and up Morgan Street. Almost five years later, on 1 June 1899, the undertaking was acquired by Dundee Corporation and saw a period of greater expansion.

Dundee City Tramways

Dundee Corporation had always owned the tracks that the Dundee & District tramcars ran on, so it made sense that the Corporation should run the tramcars too. The Corporation started an enlargement programme for the city's tram services, which saw all routes in the city electrified by the end of 1902. On 12 July 1900, the first electric tram ran from the High Street to West Park Road. This was closely followed by the Lochee and Maryfield tram routes. 1901 saw the last of the horse-drawn cars in service on the Princes Street to Baxter Park route, while the following year saw the final steam tram working from Albert Square to Fairmuir.

I mentioned in the introduction that Dundee embraced new ideas and technologies, and this was proven when, on 5 September 1912, a trolley bus service was opened along Clepington Road between Maryfield and Strathmartine Road. This venture, however, never proved to be the success it was hoped it would be. As the cars were solid-tyred vehicles, they were very hard on the uneven road surface and gave a very unsatisfactory ride along the route. The trolley bus service was abandoned on 13 May 1914 and the buses sold to Halifax Corporation.

Many of Dundee's tramcars were of the double-decked open-top type, and the cars were all gradually given top-deck covers. Much of the permanent way was also improved upon, with a lot of the track being doubled. Even during the period of the First World War, Dundee's tram system maintained its very high standards, and in the period between the wars, there was always talk of further extension due to the ever increasing number of private bus companies operating services. To combat this, Dundee Corporation started its first motor bus route between the High Street and Broughty Esplanade. Lindsay Street was the last new tram route to be opened, in 1933, but before and after then, other routes were being closed. The tramway system, however, was not allowed to fall into a state of deterioration and a considerable effort was put into rejuvenating the system. Some new tramcars were purchased, but a lot of the older cars were rebuilt to a very high standard of modern specification.

Dundee itself was changing, though, and by the 1950s, the city was growing further beyond the limitations of the tram routes. The tramcars were almost fifty years old and although they were maintained to a very high standard, they were unfortunately becoming uneconomical to maintain and repair. The nation's tram systems were becoming unfashionable and although Dundee's trams were still profitable, the decision was made to close the tram system and change over to bus operation.

Amid scenes reminiscent of a returning cup-winning football team, large crowds gathered to witness the last tram running in October 1956. Over 5,000 people turned out to see car 25, the last car, along with five others on a procession from Maryfield to Lochee Depot in the wee small hours of Sunday 21 October 1956. Only a small handful of cars survived, mainly as garden sheds and so on, but the rest of the tramcars were taken by lorry from Maryfield tram depot to a field at Marchbanks, near Beechwood, and reduced to scrap by burning. So, it was the end of an era. It its heyday, the maximum number of cars the company ran was seventy-nine; the track was a standard size of 4 feet 8.5 inches and total route mileage was thought to be about 18.5 miles.

Dundee, Broughty Ferry & District Tramways Company Limited

The Dundee, Broughty Ferry & District Tramways Company operated 4.5 miles of track with a gauge of 4 feet 8.5 inches. It ran from Monifieth and through Broughty Ferry to the Dundee boundary. Through running powers enabled cars to run to Dundee City Centre over the Corporation tracks. A section of the route was basically classed as a light railway as it ran on sleeper track through the privately owned Craigie Estate. The original twelve cars of 1905 were increased to sixteen by 1930, the year that the company was purchased by Dundee Corporation. The following year, this line was abandoned and the service was replaced by motor buses.

Walter Alexander, Alexander (Northern), Northern Scottish, Strathtay Scottish, Stagecoach

The evolution of the Walter Alexander Company in and around Dundee has, luckily, been quite straightforward and easy enough to understand and follow.

It all started in 1949, when the Dundee area of Scottish Omnibuses (SMT) was acquired, thus giving Alexander's a foothold in the area for the first time. Fifty-five buses passed over to Alexander by virtue of this takeover. The SMT themselves had only been operating in the area since they took over ownership of the Dundee Mechanical Transport Company in 1920. The SMT had been operating from a depot in Westfield Avenue, which was given the depot shed code of D2. This depot closed in the 1950s, leaving Alexander's their main depot at Seagate Bus Station. Between 1949 and 1961, Alexander's fleet of vehicles were all single-decked. This was due to the rural nature of the territory it served, with a low population density, as the city itself was well catered for by Dundee Corporation.

Popular up until 1962, the blue colour on their buses was being replaced with a very vibrant, bold shade of yellow. At this time, the bus fleet seemed to be predominantly made up of Leyland, AEC and Bedford buses. When the Alexander empire was split up in 1961, each area had its own autonomy. Because of the nature of the area, Alexander (Northern), as it was now called, updated its fleet. Dundee ended up seeing the introduction of a good few Ford vehicles and, over time, the Leyland Leopard. It also saw the introduction of one of Northern's first double deckers, the Albion Lowlander.

Things pretty much stayed the same until the Scottish Bus Group re-organisation in the late 1970s saw the company adopt the new corporate name 'Northern Scottish'. During 1980, there was a good deal of co-operation between Northern, Tayside Regional Transport and British Rail, resulting in the 'Tayway' scheme, and although used on advertising and timetables, the Tayway slogan never made it onto any of the Northern vehicles. Things remained pretty static until a further change in 1985 saw the creation of Strathtay Scottish. This company was created by merging parts of Midland Scottish and Northern Scottish along the River Tay area. The new Strathtay company adopted a striking blue and orange livery. After the privatisation of the bus industry in 1989, Strathtay came under the control of the Traction Group but changed hands once again in 2005 when it was acquired by its present owner, Stagecoach.

Dundee Corporation, Tayside Regional transport, Travel Dundee

From 1921, the City of Dundee saw motor buses being operated with the introduction of four Thorneycroft single-deckers in addition to the city's tramcars. The tram system continued to be extended until 1933, but was closed on 21 October 1956. Buses replaced the trams, and the department was renamed Dundee Corporation Transport. The Corporation's first double-deckers appeared in 1931. These were twelve Leyland Titan TD1s, which were bought to replace the Broughty Ferry trams. By 1935, after trying out several types of vehicles and demonstrators, the Corporation decided to concentrate on vehicles built on AEC and Daimler chassis.

During the early part of the 1960s, Dundee Corporation found itself on the receiving end of the trade unions' wrath after trying to introduce a number of one-man-operated buses. The fallout was resolved, and by the middle of the decade, things were back to normal. It was also about this time that the Corporation buses were appearing in a very dull looking all-over green. Newer buses like the rear engined Daimler Fleetline were appearing and they proved to be popular with the Corporation and the public alike. One type of bus that did fail was the single-decked version of the Fleetline with dual-door Alexander W-type bodywork. The bus body tended to break up early on in its life due to the 'flexibility' of the chassis for the single-deck version of the Fleetline. A few of the buses were rebodied and some even managed to make it into the next operator of the bus fleet.

In 1975, local government re-organisation saw bus operations passed over to the new Tayside Regional Council, but despite this name change, bus operations were still confined to Dundee and its suburbs. Buses were now being repainted into their new colours, consisting of two shades of blue with white as a relief colour. The bus operation was eventually restructured for privatisation and became the Tayside Public Transport Company Limited in 1986. This new company was sold to its employees in 1991, but was then sold on to the National Express Group in 1997. At first, the new company was trading as Travel Dundee, but in more recent times they changed their trade name to National Express Dundee.

Two of Dundee's finest pose for the camera around the end of the nineteenth century. This is the Nethergate at the city churches, the central location for the city's Hansom cabs, as seen behind the two police constables. The Hansom cabs were responsible, before the arrival of the tramway system, for moving the city's gentry and other upper classes from A to B.

Around the turn of the century, Dundee was pretty much like any other city of similar size and stature. This included its transport links in and around the city centre, as shown here in 1895 by two of the important means of transport at the time: the Hansom cab and the tramways. This image shows the cab stance in the city's Nethergate/High Street area. The cab fares were apparently calculated by various zones, taking the Nethergate stance as its central point.

Former Glasgow car No. 3A was one of Dundee's first horse-drawn tramcars and it is seen sitting at one of the city's first termini at the Post Office, Meadowside, in 1877. The main building, on the right hand side of the photograph, is the McManus Art Gallery and Museum. It has been at the heart of the city's culture since it opened in 1867 and is guarded by the watchful eye of the Robert Burns statue at the front. The adverts seen on the car are for 'Sinclair's cold water soap' and 'J. P. Smith & Co; 78 High Street', who were advertising the sale of men's trousers.

This horse-drawn tramcar started life as No. CIX in 1879, but was rebuilt and renumbered as No. 9 in 1889, as seen in this photograph. The location is the High Street and it is seen on a service between Morgan Hospital and Dalhousie Terrace. This was one of the tramcars that were taken over by the Corporation in 1899 after the agreement two years previously, mentioned in the introduction pages.

Also seen at the turn of the century, under Corporation control, is steam-hauled, double-deck car No. 4. It is travelling on the service between the High Street and Fairmuir to the north of the city centre and is being hauled by either steam engine 11 or 12. We know this because of the condenser seen on the roof of the steam car. The building on the extreme left is part of the McManus Art Gallery and Museum, seen in an earlier photograph.

A healthy load of passengers can be seen boarding an unknown tramcar with steam locomotive just around the corner from the previous image at Meadowside at the start of the twentieth century. Among the adverts carried by the tramcar is another for J. P. Smith & Sons of the High Street, while the others are for the more traditional Fry's Cocoa and Rising Sun stove polish.

The year 1902 saw the arrival of the single-deck 'Conshie' cars, Nos 49–54. They are captured here on arrival in Dundee having been transported north by train on low-loader wagons. These cars were used exclusively on the steep Constitution Road route between Reform Street and Hilltown, Clepington Road or Fairmuir. They were all withdrawn early in 1928 after the Constitution Road route was abandoned.

This picture shows 'crews beside single deck trams'. As the tram in the background appears to be one of the Constitution Road cars, looking in an immaculate condition, I would surmise that the image shows some of the newly acquired personnel who would be undergoing training for their roles as drivers and conductors, in preparation for the service using the new Constitution Road cars.

Taking a peek inside Central Depot, situated just off Lochee Road, we find three of the Constitution Road (Conshie) cars sitting awaiting their turns of duty for the day. In the early 1920s, these single-deck cars eventually ended up working out of Maryfield Depot. This was due to the need for increased space for the repair work carried out at the Central Depot at the time.

Turning our attention to Maryfield Depot, we see the plain track layout and the locations of the pits for working underneath the tramcar chassis. The tramcars seen in this photograph were built by Dick Kerr in 1900–01, but by 1907 the top decks had been covered. By the time of the publication of this book, Maryfield Depot should be open as the new home for Dundee Museum of Transport. It is quite fitting that such a place as this should be used for such a purpose, as we see trams and buses once again in a building that was intended for them.

Here we see an off-side view of one of the Dick Kerr trams at the Pillars before any new top deck cover was fitted. You can clearly see the 'scissors' type of gate at the driving end of the car to stop passengers from entering or leaving on that side. It would be opened when the tramcar was travelling in the opposite direction. Basically, passengers could only board or alight on the pavement side of the road to prevent any accidents from happening.

THE FIRST SUNDAY CAR AT NINEWELLS, DUNDEE, 10TH SEPT, 1905.

As the caption on this postcard says, it shows the first Sunday tramcar at Ninewells on 10 September 1905. After being knocked back two years previously, permission was given to operate Sunday services in this year. On this first day of service, the cars only operated between 10 and 11 a.m., and 12.10 and 9.10 p.m. so as not to cause any disturbance during church services. I would guess that the tramcar shown here was conveying passengers to or from one of the local church services mentioned.

This old postcard image shows a rather busy High Street around 1900 as people make their way around the city centre. There is no denying the fact that the trams played a major role in allowing people to travel from the out-lying areas at a reasonable, cheap price. Two or three horse-drawn carts are seen to be the only other form of transport on the High Street at this time.

It is only a couple of years later than the previous photograph, but here we see the arrival of one of the newly covered tramcars. This afforded the upper deck at least a degree of comfort as it offered shelter from the wind and rain. The arches of the Town House, seen here on the right of the postcard, offered shelter to the tramway men as this was the timing and crew changing point for all routes. Built in 1734, this fine building was demolished in 1932.

This photograph was taken in 1895, and shows permanent way staff undertaking repairs to the tramline in Hilltown. Little time was wasted over a century ago and repairs were usually carried out quite quickly, causing as little disruption to the system as possible. Nowadays, so much planning would have to be carried out in regards to health and safety, as well as coping with the large volume of traffic on the road.

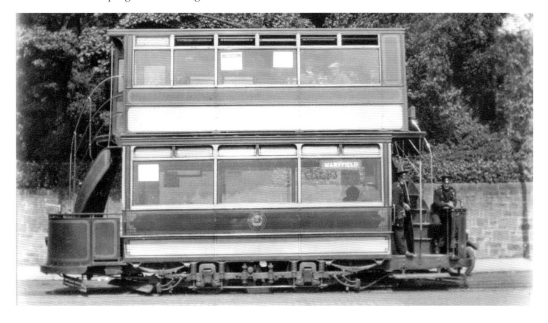

One of the Dick Kerr four-wheeled trams is shown here, giving us a good broadside view of this type of car after it was fitted with covers. The ends of the upper deck were initially left open but were later enclosed, as shown on this car. We also get a good view of the chassis arrangement and the 'lifeguard'. The lifeguard is the slotted arrangement below the driver's position that prevented unwary pedestrians from being run over.

An extremely busy-looking High Street can be seen here in this image, probably taken in the 1930s. Trams, cars, lorries, bikes and horses and carts all seem to be jostling for position while trying to avoid pedestrians in the street as the city centre prepares for the day's trading to commence. It is good to see an old established company such as Burton, on the right in the image, still going strong today.

Another broadside view of another Dick Kerr-built tram. This one is decorated primarily with holly, but other items such as silver bells, coloured lights and other baubles can be seen as adornments. This was a treat from the tramway men to the bairns of the City of Dundee at Christmas time. Usually driven by 'Santa Claus', it was a free ride on the tramcar that the kids used to look forward to and enjoy very much. The window notice reads: 'The tramwaymen's treat to the bairns'.

Right: This image shows one of the twelve tramcars belonging to the Dundee, Broughty Ferry & District Tramways Company. Car No. 10 is seen here at the terminus in Monifieth High Street. These cars were built by the Brush Electrical Engineering Company of Loughborough and were generally similar to those being used in Dundee.

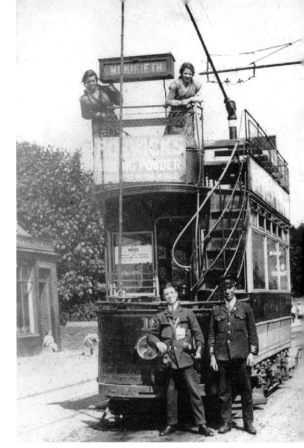

Below: This old colourised postcard image dating from 1906 shows one of the Dundee, Broughty Ferry & District tramcars sitting at the terminus in Monifieth. The line between Dundee and Monifieth was principally double track, but there were three locations between Monifieth and Barnhill where the line was only single track. The line between Dundee and Monifieth closed on 15 May 1931.

High Street, Monifieth

A busy scene in Dundee Meadowside as three tramcars seem to be taking on a substantial amount of passengers. Car No. 23 is taking up the rear and affords us a good view of the entrance area. It was renumbered as 38 in 1924 but was deemed 'surplus to requirements' as other cars in the fleet were modernised. It was subsequently scrapped in 1931.

Meadowside is once again the location as we see car No. 27 and an unidentified stable-mate going about their business around the turn of last century. The buildings in this area remain largely unchanged, with the Trades Bar building on the far corner and the old Royal Hotel on the nearest corner. Note the decorative shield on the awning over the entrance to the hotel. Like the car in the previous photograph, this was also scrapped, being broken up in 1932.

Another of the iconic locations in Dundee is known as the 'Sinderins'. This is the junction where Hawkhill meets Perth Road. A local bobby is seen standing on duty on the corner as a tramcar makes its way towards its terminus at Ninewells. A few of the buildings seen in Hawkhill, and on the corner, have been demolished over the years, but today the area is still well served by local transport.

Car No. 19 is caught in the sun as it sits in the vennel at the entrance to Lochee tram depot. On the broad cream band between decks, you can see the position of the Corporation 'roundel'. I believe this site was eventually discontinued, as it was a profitable location for the display of adverts. The gentleman on the left may be a member of the depot staff as he looks to be dressed for a more 'hands on' type of work.

The tramline through Lindsay Street was opened in 1933 and was latterly the terminus for the tram route from Lochee. A rather well-maintained, and clean, Car 25 is pictured at the tram stop below the Old Steeple as it makes its way 'around the block' to Reform Street.

By way of a comparison to the previous photograph, Car 27 is pictured at the same location, but probably by this time used as the terminus. The condition of the tramcar seems rather unkempt and grubby, which is a bit of a surprise given the reputation Dundee Corporation had for the high standards of maintenance of their vehicles.

Car 27 has just arrived at the terminus at Lochee, which was at the junction with Liff Road at St Luke's Church. Car 27 was also noted in an earlier photograph in the same rather grubby looking condition it appears here. One of the prominent front adverts carried at the time was for Weston's Biscuits, the forerunner of the company responsible for giving us the Wagon Wheel biscuit.

Lochee High Street is the location as we see tramcar No. 24 trundle downhill en route to its terminus at Reform Street. Lochee tram depot was just behind the tenements on the left, the entrance being just up from the rear of the car in the distance. Although there are now many new buildings in the High Street, Lochee remains very distinct and recognisable to this day.

Car 30 looks in immaculate condition as it sits at the terminus at Lochee adorned with a solitary side advert for the *Daily Express*. The spire of Lochee parish church looks over the treetops as if to keep a watchful eye over the suburb.

This old postcard image shows us a good view looking down a rather busy Nethergate. Three tramcars dominate the road with only a couple of period cars for company and no buses on view. Up until their final years, the tramcar pretty much dominated the streets around the city centre. It's just a pity the same couldn't be said about not just Dundee, but other city centres too nowadays.

Ninewells is the location as we find tramcar No. 44 about to embark on a journey to Maryfield to the north-east of the city during an obvious quiet period. The section of track between Ninewells and Hyndford Street was predominantly single track with the occasional passing loop.

Tramcar No. 46 has just left from the terminus on Forfar Road at Maryfield, just past the junction with Clepington Road. In a few seconds it will have passed the entrance to Maryfield tram depot, on the right-hand side of the road, as it makes its way to Ninewells. This image shows quite clearly the layout, or display, of the bus and tram stop signage.

A rather fine view of tramcar No. 46 as it makes its way along Perth Road towards its terminus at Ninewells. Adverts on display on the tramcar were typical for the time and include those for Golden Shred Marmalade and the *Scottish Daily Express*. The small advert on the bumper is promoting Gussie Park Carnival.

The buses seem to be enjoying a bit of a rest in Maryfield depot yard as tramcar No. 47 is seen to be doing all the work. Originally built in 1916 by Hurst Nelson with an extended top canopy and numbered 77, it was renumbered as 73 in 1927. It was rebuilt again in 1932 as No. 47 and is seen here in its final form.

Here we see an image of an unknown tramcar taken from a position on the railway bridge over the end of the High Street at Lochee Station. The tramcar still seems to draw the attention of the locals as it makes its way northward up Logie Street, approaching the junction at Muirton Road and Loon's Road. Many of the buildings on the main street still exist today, although many of those in the background have been demolished.

A fine broadside view of one of the tramcars I believe to be numbered somewhere in the 34–40 range. It is one of the cars built by Hurst Nelson in 1921 in the 83–90 number range, but rebuilt in 1932–33 to the specifications seen here, being renumbered in its final number range in 1936. All of the cars in this final number range were scrapped twenty years later in 1956.

This view of one of the Corporation tramcars heading down Dens Road sometime in the 1950s seems to epitomise the character associated with Dundee. The tenements remain, but the embankment area on the right behind the advertising boards is now an area of trees, bushes and various other flora.

Another busy scene in the High Street, with some of the Corporation's trams and buses going about their daily routine. Two of the businesses on show on the corner are H. Samuel and Timpson, both of which are still in their respective premises today. This area is now principally pedestrianised, with trees having been planted, giving the area a more relaxed feel about it.

It was a puzzle trying to find the exact location where this old photograph was taken. To the best of my ability and knowledge, I believe the location to be along Blackness Road, near its junction with West Park Road. It was one of the limited routes within Dundee that was single track with passing loops in certain places. Coupled with the style of the houses and the tree-lined street, it is the best I could come up with. It is interesting to note that although both cars have adverts for Red & White cigarettes, the advert on Car 11 on the left is shorter in length than the similar advert on Car 24.

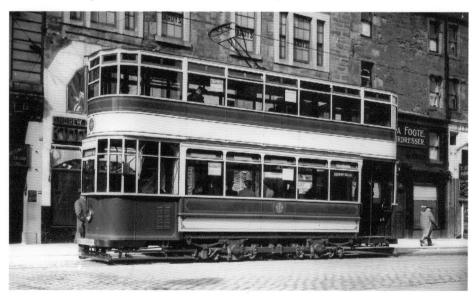

It is 1937 and Downfield-bound tramcar No. 14 sits at the stop outside one of Dundee's old, well-known businesses in the High Street, Hardy's, who sold various items of home furnishing. It is well worth noticing how clean the tramcar looks. Dundee Corporation had a well-deserved reputation for keeping their trams and buses well maintained. Posters stuck to the inside of some windows are advertising what's on at the Majestic Cinema, which was located in Seagate. At various other times, it was also known as the Capitol Cinema and the ABC.

There is something quite relaxed about the atmosphere in this photograph as two of the Corporation's tramcars are seen in Dundee High Street. An elderly gentleman surveys the scene as a female passenger boards the tramcar shortly before it makes the journey to the road end at West Park. Also of note in the photograph is the usage of the shop awnings, something that is hardly seen in modern days.

Tramcar No. 21 is caught on Lochee Road, adjacent to one of the city's well-known old features, the Polepark waiting room. Now unfortunately demolished, the area having been landscaped, it offered shelter for waiting passengers on a rainy day. Later on, it was also used as a newsagent's, as seen in this photograph here. A similar waiting room was erected at Fairmuir but was demolished many years ago.

Although hard to make out, and requiring a bit of scrutiny, this appears to be tramcar No. 23. It is in the High Street at the tram stops, which are the red coloured poles on the left-hand side. One of the Corporation's Daimler CVD6 single-deck buses makes an appearance as it turns down into Crichton Street on a local service.

A very busy Dundee High Street is seen here as shoppers go about their business. Tramcar No. 24 has just passed by as it heads northwards towards its destination of Lochee. I would imagine this was a Saturday as, upon closer inspection, two or three children can be seen with their parents. In those days, if you were off school for any reason, you weren't allowed outside.

An unidentified tramcar is seen in the passing loop at the end of West Park Road on Perth Road. This loop was also a terminus for some services running between Ninewells and the city centre. Another classic period advert for Aspro pain relief tablets is on show on the front of this car. The sharp-eyed reader will have noticed the tramcar request stops on the lamp posts.

Tramcar No. 34 invites you to 'Laugh with the Gambols' in the *Scottish Daily Express*, and to try Bovril as it makes tracks along the High Street on its route to Maryfield. Among the old establishments on show are Hardy's Furnishing Stores on the right-hand side and the Royal Dundee Institution for the Blind on the left.

The lower deck of tramcar No. 36 looks well patronised as it sits in the High Street waiting on its departure time. It would shortly be heading west towards Ninewells. Adverts displayed on the tramcar panels are for Miller Confectionery and Player's Cigarettes. Tobacco advertising was widely accepted in the days before health issues became a major concern in social attitudes.

Car 25 had the distinction of being the last tramcar to operate in service over the Dundee Corporation system. Although this postcard image shows the date of 20 October 1956, it finally ended its shift in the wee small hours of the following day. Around 5,000 people turned out to bid a sad farewell to Dundee's trams.

Between September 1912 and May 1914, Dundee had the honour of being the first city in Scotland to operate a trolleybus service. The service operated between Maryfield Depot and the Clepington Road terminus, using two single-deck vehicles with bodies by Milnes Voss on chassis by Brown of Huddersfield. They were numbered 67 and 68 in the same series as the tramcars. It must have been a very bumpy ride on those solid tyres.

A fine general view looking down the High Street in the direction of the present-day Overgate Shopping Centre. This view gives us a general impression of the track layout as well as a good selection of period road vehicles. The single-deck bus exiting from the junction appears to be one of the Corporation's Weymann-bodied Daimler CVD6s.

TOP OF HILLTOWN, DUNDEE.   A.4884.

One of the Corporation tramcars follows hot on the heels of one of the Cowieson-bodied Daimler COG6s which had served the city well for almost twenty years. Some of Dundee's earliest traffic lights can be seen on the corners of this junction at the top of Hilltown.

This is one of those rare images that let us see one of Alexander's blue buses and a Corporation tramcar together in colour. The main thing that is noticeable is the difference in height between the tramcar and the low bridge-type body on the Alexander's bus behind. Because Alexander's worked on a lot of rural routes, a lot of the rural rail bridges necessitated the used of low-height bus bodies.

Here we see Dundee High Street around 1930. One of Dundee's tramcars can be seen down the bottom end of the street in the condition before the final rebuilds took place later on during that decade. We can also see two of Dundee's first buses as a couple of Leyland Lions are also on show. These buses were new at the end of the 1920s.

A grand overall view is afforded to us of the Dock Street bus stance area in this view taken from a high vantage point. It lets us see the general layout of the stance and how busy it was, with a multitude of vehicle types on show. It must also be said that health and safety issues were a lot more relaxed about sixty years ago. (*Derek Simpson Collection*)

33

No. 149, an AEC Regent 3 with Brockhouse H30/26R bodywork, sits outside the Royal Bank of Scotland on the High Street at the junction with Castle Street. One hardy old soul looks to be asleep against the lower window, perhaps after a long day's shopping around the city centre.

A Daimler CVD6 with Brush B39R bodywork (14) is seen at rest in Crichton Street before heading out on service No. 3 to Johnston Avenue, Invergowrie. All of this batch of ten arrived new in 1951 and lasted for seventeen years with the Corporation before all being withdrawn in 1968. This was one of seven that were sold to the dealer Dunsmore of Larkhall. (*Mike Penn*)

This was a bit of an odd one for Dundee Corporation. CYJ315 (22) was an AEC Regal IV with an Alexander B39D layout. It was fitted with a fare box to operate an 'Express' service with a flat fare of 3*d* on route No. 9 to Trottick. The ordinary service fare was 2½*d*. It was also used on the 1A/1B routes to St Mary's, on which it is seen here. It was eventually sold on to a Broughty Ferry dealer in 1974. (*Derek Simpson Collection*)

When looking at this image of CYJ252 (137), I cannot help but think of Joseph and his coat of many colours. Maybe not so many colours, but definitely quite a few different shades of green are shown here. This Alexander-bodied AEC Regent 3, seen here in Dock Street getting ready to do a local school run, has survived into preservation.

Crichton Street is once again the location as we find CTS530 (21), an AEC Regal IV with Weymann B44F bodywork, ready to depart on a local service to Johnston Avenue. These buses were Dundee's first 8-foot-wide buses, the extra width perhaps playing a part in the damage to the lower front and nearside panels. (*Mike Penn*)

No. 600 was tried by Tayside before it purchased batch 1–15 in 1975. All of the vehicles in this batch were painted by Lothian prior to entering service with Tayside. The batch notoriously had a selection of Corporation green and white, and some had Tayside blue and white – all very confusing! (*Derek Simpson Collection*)

Above: CYJ254 (139) was one of a batch of 8-foot-wide AEC Regent 3 buses bought by Dundee Corporation in 1953. The bodywork is by Alexander to an H32/26R layout and looked very stylish and uncomplicated. The bus is seen turning into the Seagate and looks heavily patronised in this 1970 scene. The era is known, as the bus carries a side advert for Esso regarding the Commonwealth Games, which were held in Edinburgh in 1970. The bus was withdrawn in 1974 and sold on to a dealer in Larkhall. (*Mike Penn*)

Right: Dundee Corporation 204 provides shade for someone seated on a wall. This was a Metro-Cammell bodied Daimler CVG6, new in 1955. It made it into Tayside RC ownership and was withdrawn in 1975. A couple of the ill-starred Fleetline saloons can be seen in the background. (*Dr George Fairbairn*)

Working its way through the city centre on a local service is DYJ440 (169), a Daimler CVG6 with Metro-Cammell H32/28R bodywork. Many city transport corporations favoured the Daimler, and Dundee was no exception, with this batch of buses being Dundee's first 'tin front' Daimlers. They were introduced at the start of 1955, with this one lasting until 1976, having made it into the new Tayside Company the previous year and being renumbered as 79. (*Len Wright*)

Dock Street bus stance is the location here, as we see YJ9058 (54), a Daimler CVD6 with a Northern Counties H30/26R body, at rest between runs. It is in good company as it sits beside one of its stable-mates, YJ9054 (50). No. 54 was sold in 1966 to Smith of Dundee and saw further use as a travelling showroom, while No. 50 was transferred to the building department of the Corporation, also in 1966. (*Len Wright*)

KGK780 (239) was former London Transport AEC Regent RT1501. This was one of about thirty vehicles which were acquired from London in 1956 to be used on the tram replacement services. It is seen in the Nethergate on service 37 to the Sinderins. The year would be 1964 as we see a fantastic collection of period cars on show outside the former Playhouse Cinema, which is showing *The Slave Merchants*, a 1964 film. (*Len Wright*)

KTS99 (105) was a Daimler CVG6 with Alexander H37/28R bodywork, which was new to Dundee Corporation in 1960. This photograph was probably taken in around 1963–4 as you can see the construction of the Tay Road Bridge in the background as well as a Mk 1 Ford Cortina leading the bus along the cobbled street. (*Len Wright*)

Seen in its days as a training bus, we find YJ9127, a Weymann B35R bodied Daimler CVD6, new in 1947. Formally No. 4 in the Dundee Corporation fleet, this vehicle was withdrawn at the end of 1965 and was used until 1971 for the purpose seen here. It then saw further use with the Social Work Department for the carriage of wheelchairs, even when transferred to the new Tayside Regional Council in 1975. It was eventually sold by 1980. (*Derek Simpson Collection*)

I have a liking for Alexander's Y-type bodywork, but the version required by Dundee Corporation makes the destination display look disproportionate to the rest of the vehicle. This is CTS125D (125), an AEC Reliance bought in 1966 and seen on a local run to Claverhouse. (*Mike Penn*)

In an earlier image, we managed to see Dock Street bus stance from a high viewpoint. This image gives us the reverse but is every bit as good. Here, we are afforded a good view of various buses on stance or parked up on a layover. A couple of new Daimler Fleetlines are in the background, but we are drawn to the lead Daimler CVD6, ATS904 (124), and the wider AEC Regent 3, CYJ250 (135), beside it. (*Derek Simpson Collection*)

Dundee Corporation's love for the Daimler was continued when they decided to buy twenty Fleetline buses with Alexander high bridge J-type bodywork in 1966. CYJ847D (47) was pictured in the High Street with one of the Corporation's older half-cab Daimlers in hot pursuit. (*Mike Penn*)

This beast was an Alexander W-type bodied Daimler SRG6LX and bears the fleet number 223. KTS223H was new to Dundee Corporation in 1970, had seating for forty-six and was fitted with dual doors. Notice the gradual rise in the level of the seat backs in the windows. This type of bus must have had a sloping floor rising up from front to rear. (*Mike Penn*)

This iteration of Dundee's livery was, I thought, rather drab if dignified. It could have used a bit of white relief here or there. The Tayside blue and white that came later was much cheerier, I think. DCT 157, a 1973 Daimler Fleetline with Alexander bodywork, loads on the way out of the city centre. (*Dr George Fairbairn*)

Above: A Daimler CVG6 with Metro-Cammell body photographed in Trades Lane, Dundee, on Tuesday 16 May 1978, by which time it had become a training bus in the fleet of Tayside Regional Transport. It had been new in 1958 to what must have been Dundee Corporation. I'm puzzled by the PAYE sign on the front. (*Stephen Dowle*)

Right: This rather atmospheric photograph shows Dundee Corporation tree lopper and driver trainer YJ2792 heading up Pitkerro Road during May 1965. The bus is a Metropolitan-Cammell H27/26R-bodied Daimler COG6, and carried the fleet number 65 in service between arrival in 1936 and withdrawal in 1953. It lasted in its latter role until final withdrawal in 1966. (*Iain Farquhar*)

A further batch of five Daimler Fleetlines arrived in 1968, again with Alexander J-type H44/34F bodies, one of which was FTS884F (284). It is pictured here passing one of the W-type single-decked buses while leaving Dock Street bus stance on local service No. 18 to Kirkton. The destination display panel looks a bit simpler and better than it did on the first batch. (*Mike Penn*)

A Weymann-bodied Daimler CVG6, quite possibly FYJ786 (246), heads south-west on Pitkerro Road as the sun breaks through the haar on a summer morning in 1965. Even though the bus seems to be well patronised, it would probably be having no trouble at all in climbing the incline with the extra ton or so. (*Iain Farquhar*)

New to Walter Alexander in 1940, Alexander-bodied Leyland TS8 special WG9013 (P620) takes a well-earned rest in the layover area at Seagate Bus Station. This bus received its 'N' prefix to the fleet number in 1962, but unfortunately it was sold for scrap the following year. It is nice to see that even in 1940, Alexander's built buses with a bit of style to the body panelling. (*Paul Redmond*)

Another classic Alexander-bodied bus is AEC Regal AWG652 (A65). It is parked up just outside the entrance to the bus depot at Seagate and has recently been repainted from the old Alexander's blue to the new yellow and cream livery that was adopted by Alexander (Northern) at the split of the company in 1961. It has still to receive the 'N' prefix to the fleet number, which it did the following year (1962). Withdrawn in 1967, it was sold to Macdonald, Dundee, where it saw further use as an office for taxis. (*Paul Redmond*)

Another image showing two classic vehicles, again parked up within the confines of Seagate Bus Station. On the left we have DMS130 (NA104), a 1951 AEC Regal 3, while on the right is AWG554 (NPA19), a Leyland PS1 of 1947 vintage. Both these vehicles wear bodywork by Alexander's. NA104 was withdrawn in 1971 and was last reported as being a private bus in Southampton later that year, while NPA19 was withdrawn the previous year. (*Mike Penn*)

Another Alexander-bodied Leyland PS1, this one dating from 1949, and once again the location is the layover area at Seagate Bus Station. BWG528 (PA123) is also in the condition where it has just been repainted from blue to yellow after the 1961 split, but has still to have its fleet number changed to show the 'N' prefix. Withdrawn in 1971, it ended up at Kyre Boy's Club in 1972. (*Paul Redmond*)

There is no doubt that the Alexander-bodied Leyland PS1 was a popular choice of vehicle with the three Alexander companies. Seen here leaving Seagate bus station on service 590 to Alyth, we find CMS202 (NPA134) showing its curves to good effect. I only hope that the person that applied the poster to the rear of the AEC Reliance on the left had the good sense to cut the poster down the middle, allowing the rear boot to open. (*Mike Penn*)

In the days when you left Seagate Bus Station by the present day entrance, a rather busy Alexander-bodied AEC Regal 3, DMS126 (NA100), departs on service 19B to Carnoustie, just a short distance along the coast. The posters seen on the rear of the other buses sitting on their stances display adverts for Haig Scotch Whisky, a popular advert at the time. (*Mike Penn*)

Taking a peek inside Seagate Depot, we can see a host of various bus types on show. Prominent among them is CWG339 (NPA212). Although it is another Leyland PS1, this one has body styling by Burlingham of Blackpool. Although stylish looking to a degree, certainly for a bus of 1950 vintage, there is something not quite right about the look of this body style. This bus was withdrawn in 1971 and ended up working for a contractor in West Hartlepool. (*Paul Redmond*)

Sporting the newer style of Alexander bodywork, AEC Reliance JWG704 (AC124) is seen at rest in Seagate Bus Station. It has still to receive its 'N' fleet number prefix, like so many vehicles around 1961, but this would be rectified the following year. It was withdrawn in 1976, ending up at the (in)famous Muir's scrapyard in Kirkcaldy, the final resting place for many buses from Fife, Northern and Eastern Scottish bus companies among others. It should also be noted how clean Alexander's kept their buses around this time. (*Paul Redmond*)

Dundee's NW 270 (JRS470F) is pictured in Aberfoyle in June 1971, invariably on one of the company's tours. New in April 1968, it was a Bedford VAS5 with Duple C29F coachwork. This medium-sized coach would have had a bright, well-lit interior with the quarter lights above the passenger seating area. (*Barry Sanjana*)

Dundee's WRS652L (NT52) was one of a large fleet of Fords bought by Alexander (Northern) in the 1970s. This one, new in 1973, carried Alexander C41F bodywork on an R1014 chassis, and is seen alongside the now-disappeared Parliamentary Road in the parking area behind Buchanan Street Bus Station in Glasgow in 1976. (*Barry Sanjana*)

SRS131 (NW261) was a Bedford VAS1 with Duple C29F bodywork. It was new to Alexander (Northern) in May 1962 and based at the company's Dundee depot. It is seen here at Dock Street stance waiting for the arrival of its passengers on one of the company's famous tours. The fresh antimacassars are on the seat backs and the bus is displaying 'On Tour' on the bumper. Antimacassars were used in those days as a means of keeping hair cream, which was widely used at the time, off the upholstery. (*Paul Redmond*)

The Albion Lowlander was always considered a bit of a dud. Albion must have hoped for orders from the Scottish municipals but none were forthcoming. In England, two municipals and a handful of BET subsidiaries ordered small numbers. This left the Scottish Bus Group, which took modest numbers of the Lowlander into stock. Those examples that survived early withdrawal tended to lead a rootless existence, being transferred from company to company within the group. The vehicle in the photograph is an Albion Lowlander LR1 (pneumo-cyclic gearbox and leaf springs) with Alexander body. It had been new to the Western SMT company but served out its latter years in the fleet of Alexander Northern. It was photographed at Dundee Bus Station on Tuesday 16 May 1978. (*Stephen Dowle*)

SRS131 (NW261) is once again the subject as we find the vehicle in Seagate Bus Station carrying out some 'bread and butter' duties as it readies itself for a journey to Errol. The location is on the typical Scottish Bus Group paper destination stuck on the inside of the windscreen. You can see it in front of the driver's hat. Nowadays, you wouldn't get away with putting something like that in such a location as to block any part of the driver's view of the road, or running with an open entrance door. A fine selection of single-deckers is hiding behind the Bedford.

KRG462F (NNV 62) was an Albion Viking with Alexander's famous Y-type coach bodywork. It is seen here in Dundee Bus Station on Tuesday 16 May 1978. This type of 32-foot chassis with a VK43AL rear engine was never a common type and many were exported. On a point of note: the bluebird is a species unknown to British ornithology. It is regrettable, then, that Alexander's should have chosen this non-bird as its emblem. (*Stephen Dowle*)

URS200 (NAC219) was an AEC Reliance with an Alexander forty-one-seat coach body, new to Alexander Northern in 1963. It must therefore have been nearing the end of its life when it was photographed turning into Dundee bus station on Tuesday 16 May 1978. A couple of nice features in the photograph are the car in the background, either an Austin Cambridge or a Wolseley, but my favourite feature is the road sweeper's pneumatic-tyred dustbin carriage on the opposite pavement. (*Stephen Dowle*)

Tayside Region's training bus 3655FG (T2) was a former Alexander (Fife) vehicle that was bought by Tayside in 1979 specifically as a training bus. It was fitted out for this purpose at the Fife works in Kirkcaldy prior to handover. It appears to need a bit of bodywork repaired below the cab window, due to a learner driver's mistake perhaps. (*Paul Redmond*)

Former Edinburgh Corporation 761 was sold to Dundee just prior to the formation of the new Regional Councils, and received Dundee Corporation livery at Shrubhill before its journey north. It later entered the training fleet. It is seen here in the company of Alexander W-type Fleetline of Tayside Regional Council, and a former Alexander (Midland) Lodekka, both also driver trainers. (*Dr George Fairbairn*)

A selection of training buses sits forlornly in Dock Street depot, waiting on the next intake of trainee drivers in the mid-1970s. We see former Edinburgh Corporation Leyland PD2 OFS761 (T5), and Dundee's own CVG6 Daimlers ETS976 (T1) and HTS279 (T2) wearing a mixture of liveries, with new vinyls merely having been placed over the old Corporation coat of arms on the green vehicles. (*Derek Simpson Collection*)

A fine study of two of Tayside's Alexander-bodied Daimler Fleetlines showing the contrasting bus liveries between the old and the new. Surprisingly, GYJ488G (288) on the right is older than GYJ401G (301) as they were new in 1968 and 1969 respectively. One would have imagined the lower number plate would be the older bus. These buses were photographed during the splendid summer of 1975. (*Derek Simpson Collection*)

This sad object was former Dundee Corporation CTS 529, a Weymann-bodied AEC Reliance. Here it is seen at Tayside Regional Council's Dock Street yard, being cannibalised. It had been sold out of service to the Transport & General Workers' Union. (*Dr George Fairbairn*)

Not much is known about this little bus other than the fact that it was first registered when new to Dickson of Dundee in January 1952. We also know that it was an Austin K8CVC with Plaxton Venturer C14F bodywork. It was with Dickson for four years before being sold to another operator, Hardie of Melrose. This cute little coach apparently still survives to this day in a museum somewhere in the Netherlands.

Tayside Regional Transport's LWS504 (5) was a Leyland Titan PD2/20 with MCW Orion bodywork. This was one of a batch acquired from Edinburgh Corporation. By the time LWS504 was ready to go, Dundee Corporation Transport had become Tayside Regional Transport and Edinburgh Corporation Transport was Lothian Region Transport. Tayside selected a very cheerful white and two-tone blue livery that was much brighter than the previous green and white. On a test run prior to delivery, bus No. 5 shows off its new colours, legal lettering and fleet numbers, but without the fleet names, on Inverleith Row, Edinburgh, in 1975. (*Dr George Fairbairn*)

This type of Alexander-bodied Leyland Leopard was show earlier in this book when with the old Dundee Corporation. It looked rather drab then, but the lighter colours of the newer Tayside Regional Transport department have done wonders for the overall appeal of the vehicle (apart from the repositioning of the number plate). CTS134D (229) was captured here on a shoppers' trip in the city centre. (*Clive A. Brown*)

CTS134D (229) is again the subject of this photograph and affords us a good view of the off-side of the vehicle, showing the rather strange positioning of the Tayside Region vinyls. I would have thought that below window number two would have been a good location for its application. I also believe the body style of the Scottish Bus Group Y-types looked a lot better with the aluminium waistband strips. (*Clive A. Brown*)

A very atmospheric and moody sky dominates this image of short wheelbase Seddon Pennine XVU336M (311). This unique twenty-seven-seated little vehicle must have felt rather weird to drive with such a short length. It was new to SELNEC (Manchester) in 1973 and found its way to Tayside Regional Transport before being allegedly exported to Antigua. (*Clive A. Brown*)

JUG355N (224) was a Tayside Regional Transport short Bristol LHS with ECW bodywork, purchased from West Yorkshire PTE in the late 1970s after a very short life there. It is seen turning into the Seagate, bound for the city centre despite what is shown on the blind. One of Tayside's Ailsa buses can be seen in the background in hot pursuit. (*Clive A. Brown*)

It is beyond me why Tayside Regional Transport needed to put 'In' and 'Out' above the only entry and exit door on this Alexander-bodied Daimler Fleetline. GYJ399G (299) does appear to look a bit overdone with vinyls asking for 'Exact Change Please' and 'Pay As You Enter' notices. The letter 'N' above the driver's side of the windscreen denoted a vehicle belonging to Marchbanks depot. This was classified as 'Northern', hence the use of this letter.

New in 1968 to Dundee Corporation and given the fleet number 295, Daimler Fleetline GYJ495G with Alexander J-type bodywork has now been converted for use as a training vehicle with new fleet number T4. It has been caught beside stable-mate GYJ493G on a fine sunny day in August 1981, during a quiet spell in new trainee driver intakes perhaps. (*Clive A. Brown*)

Originally, this type of single-deck Daimler chassis was fitted with Cummins 6-cylinder engines; however, it appears that by 1970, when the vehicle in the photograph was new, a Gardner engine option was being offered in an attempt to propitiate the industry's chief engineers, especially in Scotland. The photo was taken on 26 June 1979 and shows KTS22H (220) hard at work as it travels down the Nethergate on a local circular service. (*Stephen Dowle*)

The original appearance of this batch of saloon Fleetlines. The Alexander W-type body shows little sign of the stresses it was suffering. When Tayside Regional Council inherited the buses, it tried various measures to improve their structural strength. Two had the rear end rebuilt with a Fleetline bustle, this one by the Council and another by Alexander's. Many of the others had the rear bench seat removed and strapping applied to the body structure. (*Dr George Fairbairn*)

LES46P was one of Tayside Regional Council's first purchases. It is pictured here wearing the fleet number 109, but was originally issued the fleet number 72. The 1976 batch of Volvo Ailsa B55s was all bodied by Alexander with the AV-type of body but with a dual door. No. 109 is seen passing Sugarhouse Wynd, which is just off Seagate. (*Clive A. Brown*)

Exact Fare Only ... Pay As You Enter ... Tayside Regional Council were telling 'em straight at Dundee on Tuesday 26 June 1979. Change was, of course, one of the big headaches of a bus driver's job, dependent as he was for his supply of coin on passengers who always expected to be able to tender high. It could be very exasperating. The vehicle seen here was of the relatively rare long wheelbase version of the Bristol VRT, the VRTLL, with Gardner engine and Alexander body. A Volvo Ailsa with identical bodywork is seen waiting patiently behind. (*Stephen Dowle*)

Again, the rather uncommon long-wheelbase version of the Bristol VRT (VRTLL), here with Gardner 6LXB engine and bodywork by Alexander, is seen in the fleet of Tayside Regional Council. The VRT, endemic throughout England and Wales, got off on the wrong foot in Scotland. The Scottish Bus Group couldn't get on with them at all and soon fobbed them off on the National Bus Company, which was only too happy to exchange them for older Bristol FLFs. The SBG never touched them again. Perhaps these Dundee examples were the only VRTs in Scotland. The photograph was taken in Nethergate High Street, Dundee, on Tuesday 26 June 1979. (*Stephen Dowle*)

A plethora of chassis type and Alexander bodywork is on view in this photograph taken in Dock Street depot in August 1981. On view are various Daimler Fleetline, Volvo Ailsa and Bristol VRT buses, all with their variations on the popular Alexander body design at the time. The Ailsa nearest the camera was apparently used as a training vehicle for a short time before returning to PSV use. (*Clive A. Brown*)

Above: A pair of the well-kept 'PYJ—L' Daimler Fleetline/Alexander dual-door, semi-auto gearbox buses, pictured on the parking apron at Dock St depot (now much reduced in size). They were new in 1973 to Dundee Corporation, numbered 142–166, and were used on the St Mary's group of services operating north from the city centre and passing the Marchbanks depot, operated at the time of the photo by Tayside Regional Council towards the end of their short life there. There were a further fifteen similar later GSL—N reg buses (107–121, later renumbered 167–181) which had fully-auto gearboxes. Their delivery had been much delayed by the three-day week in 1973/74 and they proved to be hugely unreliable. Some of the PYJ batch graduated to the Scottish Bus Group's Fife fleet when still quite young. (*Clive A. Brown*)

Left: Tayside Regional Council had twenty-five of these long Bristol VRT buses with Alexander bodywork. OSR199R (199), seen here in Dock Street in 1981, started working from Marchbanks depot on the 15/17 Whitfield/City/Menzieshill services. They were apparently unreliable buses and were soon displaced from front line work, but not before the top deck of this bus was burnt out in a vandal attack. This one was reconfigured as a coach, but even that did not prevent its later sale, with some sister buses, to Burnley & Pendle. (*Clive A. Brown*)

DSR133V (233) was a Marshall Camair-80 rebodied Daimler Fleetline that had started off with an Alexander W-type body. My understanding was that the original body was not able to cope with the inherent flex of the chassis, hence this modification. Once again, the gradual rise in the seat level can still be seen on this Daimler chassis model. (*Clive A. Brown*)

Another Alexander-bodied Daimler Fleetline on show is PYJ460L (160). It is seen sitting in the city's Nethergate wearing the 'Tayway' branding before departing further up the coast to the seaside town of Monifieth. This initial version of Tayside livery was, in my humble opinion, the best version, as it was plain, clean and simple looking, making it quite pleasing to the eye. (*Clive A. Brown*)

In 1980 Tayside Region Transport had the use of BCK706R, a Leyland B15 built as a demonstrator in 1977. It bore the fleet number 100 during its sojourn on Tayside. This was the first B15 to wear the 'Titan' name badge. This bus was primarily used on services 15/17 (Whitfield/Ninewells Hosp.) during its sojourn at Tayside. (*Dr George Fairbairn*)

Carrying an all-over commemorative livery for The Boys Brigade, we see Volvo Ailsa B55-10, DSP935V (35), with Alexander bodywork, which was new in June 1980 to Tayside Regional Council. It is seen just over three years later in Dock Street depot during August 1983. (*Iain Lawson*)

Above: In 1970 Dundee Corporation Transport bought a batch of twenty-five Alexander W-bodied Daimler Fleetlines. Unfortunately, the flexible propensities of the chassis did not mate well with that body (nor others of the time, either). In 1980 some of them were rebodied by Marshall with their startling Camair 80 body. (*Dr George Fairbairn*)

Right: On 29 September 1984 a Tayside Region Volvo Ailsa makes its way up Lochee Road, still lined by tramway overhead standards nearly 28 years after the trams last ran. HSR39X (39) was only three years old when photographed wearing Tayside livery, which I believe suited this type of bus. (*Neale Elder*)

Tayside Regional Transport's open-air depot at Dock Street is once again the location as we find a pair of Ailsa buses with different body types on show. A84SSP (84), new in 1983 with an H48/36F East Lancs body, and WTS268T (268), new in 1979 with the more common Alexander AV body, make a fair comparison of body styles between the two manufacturers of bus bodies.

The madder stickers with the legal lettering and the crest between the doors show that this is not quite what it seems. In 1976 Tayside Regional Council 313 was loaned to Lothian for evaluation, and is seen here on the latter's service 23, passing down Trinity Road approaching the Lennox Row terminus. I don't know what LRT made of the Ailsa, save to say that no orders were forthcoming. (*Dr George Fairbairn*)

A pair of Tayside Regional Council Volvo Ailsas parked up awaiting service in Dock Street during 1979. NSP313R (113) was used extensively as a demonstrator when new and is seen wearing a wrap-round advert for Rembrand building supplies. Note the central position on the front grille of the Ailsa badge. (*Dr George Fairbairn*)

Former Tayside Volvo Ailsa LES44P was sold to Tayside Police and is seen here in the livery and condition it adopted when in their use. It seems to have been used more as an information bus, but no doubt may have been used for other purposes, such as a mobile command centre. (*Davie Stewart Collection*)

WTS272T was new to Tayside Regional Transport in 1979 with the fleet number 272. It is one of the company's Mk 2 Ailsa buses with the much suited Alexander AV type of body. Apparently, it sustained roof damage early on in its life and the decision was made to convert it to an open-topped vehicle. It is pictured here in July 1996 in Crichton Street taking on a good load of sightseers on a rare, bright summer day. (*Barry Sanjana*)

It is quite hard to keep up with the various livery differences applied to the Tayside fleet in the mid-1990s. The livery on Volvo B55 HSR49X (49) is predominantly off-white or cream, with dark blue roof and lower body, and shows no light blue at all. I think this version of the livery suited the Alexander RV type of body quite well. This bus is passing the former ABC Cinema in Seagate as it heads towards Whitfield on service 15. (*Barry Sanjana*)

Here we see Plaxton-bodied Volvo B6 M117XSR (117) as it starts to load up in Crichton Street while on service 2. This bus wears the cream and darker blue colours, but has a touch of duck egg blue on the top panel as part of a route branding for service 4. Little has changed in Crichton Street today with the exception of newer, more modern bus sheltering. (*Barry Sanjana*)

East Lancs-bodied Scania K410MSL (110) is practically empty as it makes its way along the Seagate, passing an old established public house, The Bush. It was new to Tayside Regional Transport in 1993 and is caught on camera here three years later in July 1996. It is unknown to me if the advertising slogan on the side of the bus, 'Go On, Hop On', ever had the desired effect or helped to encourage people to use the bus more often. (*Barry Sanjana*)

This Mk 2 Ailsa, CSL614V (14) with the stylish Alexander AV bodywork, is passing another old, established pub, The Hansom Cab, on the corner of Seagate and Commercial Street on a lovely sunny day during July 1996. The dark blue in the bus livery well matches the blue colour of the public house and the upper part of the shop front further down the street. There is still a pub on this corner, but it is now called Tickety Boo's. (*Barry Sanjana*)

A82SSP (82) was another Volvo B55, but this one had bodywork by East Lancs. I personally don't think that the East Lancs style of body suited the Volvo or Ailsa chassis as the windows looked too small given the hefty-looking appearance of the grille area. But that's just my opinion. The yellow board on the grille displays the legend 'Pay as You Enter'. This bus is heading out to Ninewells on the popular and often busy service 22.

SRS519K (NT19) was an Alexander Y-type-bodied Ford R226 which was bought in 1971. This type of body looked really pleasing to the eye when liveried in such a bold colour as this. This was the bus version of the Y-type, with small windows, very different when compared to the sloping panoramic windows on the coach body alongside. (*Clive A. Brown*)

Daimler Fleetline UMS89J (NRF8), with an Eastern Coach Works body, was new in 1970 to Alexander (Midland) as their MRF89. It was eventually transferred to Alexander (Northern) and is seen here with a wrap-around advert for the Clydesdale Bank as it sits in the layover area in the bus station. The window sticker pronounces that there are 'Revised fares now in operation'. (*Paul Redmond*)

I must confess I am unsure as to the reason for the spotlights attached to the rear of Albion Viking GRG428E (NNV28). This was one of a batch of buses that were bodied by Potter of Belfast, a subsidiary company of Alexander's, and this image affords us a rare view of the rear end of such an Albion Viking. It is seen facing towards the depot at Seagate, and it can be seen with the company trade plates on show. As it appears to be an Elgin-based vehicle, could it perhaps have broken down somewhere in the region and required a tow? (*Clive A. Brown*)

VST755L (NPE59) should be typical of an Alexander-bodied Leyland Leopard of 1973 vintage. This was new to Highland Omnibuses, but I believe came to Northern with several others in exchange for Ford chassis buses. This one looks unusual due to the fact it has been re-seated with bus seats, perhaps to increase the passenger capacity from forty-nine to fifty-three. The location is Seagate Bus Station. (*Paul Redmond*)

This is a typical scene from Dundee bus station in the 1980s as buses from all three former Alexander companies make use of the facilities. Notice the difference between the waistbands of the Northern and Fife vehicles, with Northern retaining the stepped waistband and the Fife Leopard wearing a straight waistband. These waistbands were purely for cosmetic purposes but did enhance the look of the Y-type body compared to the ones the old Dundee Corporation had. (*Clive A. Brown*)

The stances at Dundee's Seagate bus station as seen from the boarding platform side on 29 August 1985. The bus station was always an easy place to reach coming from Fife, and I would imagine, being near the river, it would be easy to reach from the east and west too. It is still a busy bus station and a major hub for the express services provided by Citylink and Stagecoach today. (*Neale Elder*)

USO167S (NT167) travels west along South Marketgait as it makes its way towards Wormit, via Newport, on the Fife side of the Tay. This vehicle has the traditional Alexander Y type of bodywork and is built on a Ford chassis and was new to Alexander (Northern) in 1977. It seems to be a well-patronised service and it must have been warm inside the bus as both of the skylights have been opened to aid the circulation of cool air. (*Paul Redmond*)

The Leyland Leopard with Alexander T-type body was a bus designed for medium range work and was well suited for services such as this. CRS66T (NPE66) seems to gleam in the sun as it enters Seagate Bus Station with only a small handful of shoppers on board. When kept clean, the yellow and cream livery certainly stood out among the more mundane liveries adopted by some companies in the 1980s. (*Clive A. Brown*)

Former Alexander (Midland) Daimler Fleetline UMS90J (NRF9) with ECW bodywork is pictured in Seagate, just past the bus station, as it prepares for service on a local route. There appears to be an inspector standing in the doorway, talking to an employee. I just hope nobody was in any trouble for running early, or any ticket irregularities. Once again, this is a good example of the standard of cleanliness achieved by the staff at Alexander's, not just in Dundee, but throughout their various companies. (*Clive A. Brown*)

Another good photograph here as we see the nearside profile of another of the T-type Leyland Leopards used by Northern Scottish in the 1980s. JSA105V (NPE105) was new at the start of the decade, when the company was still Alexander (Northern). It is parked up at Seagate Bus Station layover area, apparently in readiness for tour work. It is yet another example of the standard of cleanliness achieved by the company. (*Paul Redmond*)

Taking a well-earned rest in between runs, we find Albion Viking KRG459F (NNV59), with the usual Y-type body, parked up at the layover at Seagate. As pointed out in a few of the previous captions, the cleanliness of all the vehicles seen here must be mentioned. The only thing that disappoints is the marks on the grille where there had previously been fleet number and shed plates, only to be replaced by the not so convincing application of the new combined information below the grille. (*Clive A. Brown*)

NFS178Y (278) sits out in a shower of rain in Dundee Seagate bus station on Saturday 2 July 1988. It had just made the arduous journey on the Fife Scottish service No. 41 from its home depot in the Fife coastal town of Kirkcaldy. This bus was a Leyland Leopard with a dual-purpose Alexander T-type body, which was the ideal combination for longer distance journeys such as this. (*Gary Seamarks*)

Queen Mary HCD363E pauses beside former London Transport Routemaster, RM45 at Strathtay's Dundee bus station depot in March 1988. It was assumed that the former Southdown Queen Mary had ventured south from a northern area; in fact, I am sure this training vehicle was actually based in Aberdeen. Perhaps it was a nice day for a drive and the instructor just let a new trainee drive down to the city bus depot. (*Gary Seamarks*)

Strathtay training vehicle ACA230A had obviously been out and about with a new bunch of hopeful drivers when it was seen in Dundee Seagate bus station in March 1988. This bus was a former Crosville vehicle dating from 1958, but it must have been a good vehicle to have lasted the thirty years to the time of this photograph. It was last seen with an unknown owner in Germany in 1994. (*Gary Seamarks*)

VLT298 (SR2) was a Strathtay Scottish AEC Routemaster double-deck bus, acquired from London Transport. It is seen here in Crichton Street in the city centre. Compare and contrast the liveries applied to the Routemasters in this shot and the next. Not sure either really suits the bus. The stripes probably work best though. (*Clive A. Brown*)

WLT151 (SR22) was another Strathtay Scottish AEC Routemaster double-deck bus acquired from London Transport, and is wearing the alternative version of the livery shown in the previous photograph. The location for this photograph is Dundee High Street. (*Clive A. Brown*)

This beast is an AEC Matador, as used by Strathtay to attend any breakdowns. The date is March 1988 and Q684PES is seen in the vicinity of Seagate, although probably not attending to any breakdown as it appears to be driven by a driver and not a member of the engineering staff. This vehicle apparently survives in preservation to this day. (*Gary Seamarks*)

Former Alexander (Northern) Leyland Leopard GSO85V (535) passes the former ABC cinema in Seagate on a beautiful sunny day sometime during July 1996. This service looks devoid of any passengers and, unlike other services at the time, it is a one-man-operated service. It must be noted that the depot staff must have taken pride in their work going by the cleanliness of the vehicle. (*Barry Sanjana*)

Travelling west along the Nethergate on a run to Ninewells Hospital is Leyland Tiger A112ESA (501). It has the Alexander P-type body and was new to Alexander (Northern) as their NT12 in 1983. It passed to the then-new Strathtay Company when the Scottish Bus Group restructured in 1985.

M307XSN (307) was a Dennis Dart with Northern Counties bodywork, and was purchased by Strathtay Scottish in March 1995. The Dennis Dart was classed as a Midibus and was thought to be more suitable for larger towns than city work. It is seen while operating the service across the Tay Bridge to Wormit in the Kingdom of Fife. (*Barry Sanjana*)

Seen parked up at the layover area in Dundee bus station, we find Strathtay Dennis Dart K301MSN (301). It has Wright bodywork but the Strathtay livery, as applied here in July 2004, does not do anything to enhance the appearance of this vehicle. Perhaps once the vinyls have been applied? (*Suzy Scott*)

The ABC cinema in the Seagate is once again the backdrop as we see former Alexander (Northern) Leyland Olympian TSO26X (908), with ECW bodywork, hard at work on a run to Ninewells Hospital on the 73A service. Some services were obviously still worked with conductors, as witnessed here in July 1996. (*Barry Sanjana*)

On the same day as the previous image, Optare Metrorider N149DSL (149) looks rather smartly turned out as it too takes a rest between turns around the town on the 76 service. This bus was later moved on to work for Stagecoach in Perth. (*Suzy Scott*)

Commercial Street is the location for this photograph of Volvo B7 SP51AWX (703) with East Lancs bodywork. This bus had just recently been fitted with a new LED display when pictured in June 2004 on a service 73 between Dundee and Arbroath. (*Suzy Scott*)

Sidlaw Executive M688TDB. The latest operator of the Dundee High playing field shuttle service, and the latest double decker to work the run, this ex-Stagecoach Dennis Dragon originated in Kenya but spent most of its working life in Manchester, where its capacity was useful on Magicbus services. (*Chris Forbes*)

S279AOX (0279) was an Optare Solo brought up to Dundee under National Express ownership. It was new to West Midlands in 1999 at their Wolverhampton depot and came north early in 2006. It has since moved on to J. P. Minicoaches of Forfar, and more recently to Bennett of Kilwinning. It is seen here making its way through the city centre on an empty movement. (*Barry Sanjana*)

March 2003 finds that Dennis Dart SLF R87GNW (87), a recent transfer from Travel West Midlands, had been painted all-over blue, apart from the front (which has mucked up the colour balance on this photo!) for Cash Generator. The bus was sitting in the High School bus stop at Albert Square to allow another service to pick up before moving into the shared stop. (*Suzy Scott*)

For a while, it was quite common to see non-driver trainees doing learner work. Travel Dundee's R162TSR (162) is seen turning from St Andrews Street into Seagate on a quiet-looking winter's day during February 2003. This bus was a Wright-bodied Volvo B6LE and was new to the company in 1998. (*Suzy Scott*)

As you will no doubt begin to see, there seems to be an overabundance of buses with specific route branding on them. Wright-bodied Volvo P136KSL (7136) is one such example and is seen in Crichton Street on service 17 to Whitfield. This service branding has been called the 'Whitfield Hopper' and runs between Whitfield and Ninewells Hospital. (*Barry Sanjana*)

During June 2002, Travel Dundee's East Lancs-bodied Scania K410MSL (110) can be seen at Albert Square while out on service 29 between Douglas and Charleston. This bus was new to Tayside Regional Transport in 1993 and is seen here wearing an all-over sky blue livery for 'Wellgate Window Design'. (*Suzy Scott*)

Just before the arrival of Travel Dundee's Wright Gemini-bodied Volvo B7s, the Alexander-bodied version was still hard at work, as seen here in the summer of 2004. ST02MZO (181), wearing branding for the 22/22C route, is seen at the Royal Exchange Building in Albert Square on the 29 service to Douglas. (*Suzy Scott*)

The Seagate is the location for this Wright Eclipse-bodied Volvo B7TL double-decker. It Is SP54CHC (7017) and has been branded for the company's 22/22C PrimeLine service which, as can be seen on the side of the bus, runs from Ninewells Hospital, through the city centre to Downfield and Craigowl Estate. (*Barry Sanjana*)

SP54CGV (7013) is another one of the Wright/Volvo combination favoured by the National Express Group. This one, also seen operating on the company's PrimeLine service 22 to Downfield, is seen outside Primark on the High Street in June 2009 wearing an all-over side advert for the Scottish Hydro Electric Company. (*Barry Sanjana*)

My third offering for the same Wright/Volvo combination is included to show yet another variation on the company's livery. SP54CHF (7001) displays a livery with red and off-white, but now has no blue colour to show on this version. This bus is being used on service 15, which operates between the city centre and Whitfield via Pitkerro Road but is seen taking a couple of minutes' rest in Whitehall Street. (*Barry Sanjana*)

Wright Liberator-bodied Volvo B10L P125KSL (7125) is another bus displaying specific route branding, in this case for the service 32 'Fintry Shuttle'. It seems to be the usual practice with route branded buses in Dundee to show the line of route on the vehicle side somewhere. The route, as the name implies, runs between the City Centre and Fintry, taking in Maryfield and Stobswell en route. (*Barry Sanjana*)

R161RSN (7161), a Wright Renown-bodied Volvo B10BLE, sits at the bus stop in Whitehall Street awaiting its departure time. As it shows on the destination display, it will be heading to Lochee via South Road on service 28 with only a handful of weary travellers on board. Was service 28 ever given the route branding treatment? (*Barry Sanjana*)

Wright-bodied Volvo B7L Y722CJW (7067) is seen here on a local service 29 to Charleston via South Road on a wet day in June 2009. An East Lancs-bodied Stagecoach double-decker is in hot pursuit as both buses leave the bus stop outside the Yates's Wine Lodge in Seagate. This bus was new to West Midlands in 2001, but soon found its way up north due to internal bus movements within National Express. (*Barry Sanjana*)

Although intended for Western Buses, three of these Scanias arrived at Dundee depot as cover for the native ADL E400s, which headed down to London for the Olympics. SF12HWN (15815) is seen on its first day in service with Stagecoach Strathtay as it travels along Seagate on service 73 to Ninewells Hospital. (*Chris Forbes*)

Now branded for the service 57, this bus was barely two months old when it found itself helping out in London during the Olympic Games in 2012. Now settled in back home in its own territory, SP12CFV (10003), an Alexander Dennis Enviro 400, makes light work of the route between Dundee and Perth via Blairgowrie, even with a journey time just short of two hours. (*Chris Forbs*)

Seen travelling westward along Seagate is PSU374 (21124), a Wright Renown-bodied Volvo B10BLE. The registration number is a private Strathtay one and has been seen on other buses in the area at various times. It is seen here during August 2012, just after leaving the bus station on service 79A to Monikie via Broughty Ferry and Monifieth, with a journey time of about fifty minutes. (*Chris Forbes*)

S349SWF (42234) is a Plaxton-bodied Mercedes Benz minibus with seating for thirty-one persons. It was new to Yorkshire Traction in 1998, but ended up at Strathtay due to the previous owners, Traction Group, doing some vehicle movements between group companies. In January 2013, this bus was photographed here in Whitehall Street while operating on service 75 between Ethiebeaton Park and the city centre. (*Chris Forbes*)

A lot of newer vehicles in the Stagecoach fleet have started appearing on the streets without the traditional front yellow and blue 'whoosh' stripes. This may be in keeping with the design of the Enviro series of single-deck buses. One such example of the livery variation can be seen on SF04VFS (47068) as it makes its way to the city centre on service 75 from Ethiebeaton Park. (*Chris Forbes*)

This cut-down Eastern Coach Works-bodied Leyland Atlantean was an unusual-looking recovery wagon. It was new to Ribble Buses in 1979, but between then and its arrival with Stagecoach Strathtay, I must confess to knowing nothing of its history. It is included here purely due to its unique role as a recovery vehicle. (*Chris Forbes*)

Alexander Dennis ALX400 XM55KOV (18351) is taking a well-earned break late on in the evening of 22 June 2008 when photographed outside the depot entrance at Seafield. It had recently made the journey north from Stagecoach Manchester, where it had served for three years from new in 2005. For a while this type of vehicle was the main double-deck workhorse for many Stagecoach subsidiaries, and still is in some places. (*Chris Forbes*)

Pictured on the same day as the previous photograph is M151FGB (21051). It was a Volvo B10B with Wright bodywork and came to Strathtay in around 2004–5 from Stagecoach Western. It was new in 1995 to A1 (Docherty, Irvine) and registered M1ABO, and stayed with that consortium as they were absorbed by Stagecoach, although somewhere along the line it had its registration changed before it came to Dundee. It is pictured here parked up in front of the layover bays at Seagate bus station. (*Chris Forbes*)

Alexander Dennis-bodied MAN 18.240 SP08DCY (22572) is captured here on an unspecified local service. The unfortunate thing about digital cameras and the dot matrix system is that sometimes a display can disappear due to the flicker rate of the display screen. The location is Crichton Street at stance C1, and the bus is just waiting on the time for departure to arrive. (*Chris Forbes*)

The Volvo B10M with Alexander PS-type bodywork was always a popular choice of vehicle with drivers all over. This one, R927XVM (20927), was first registered with Greater Manchester in 1997 and eventually ended up with Stagecoach at Perth. However, it is seen in the Nethergate on service 42 for Tayport, meaning it probably originated from Crichton Street in the city centre. (*Chris Forbes*)

East Lancs-bodied Volvo B7TL ST52NTM (16925) is seen here on one of its normal runs, sitting at its terminus in Whitehall Street in the city centre. It is seen on service 74, which is a weekday-only service, running from this terminus to Broughty Ferry further up the coast. New in 2002 to Strathtay, it is proving to be a long-serving member of the Strathtay fleet. (*Chris Forbes*)

M305DGP (16405) was a Northern Counties-bodied Volvo Olympian that came to Strathtay from Fife. Prior to that, it had spent the early part of its career with Selkent, and Stagecoach when they took over that operation. The driver waits patiently as his bus begins to load with passengers either heading home from a day's shopping, or perhaps off to Ninewells Hospital for an appointment, or visiting a loved one. (Chris Forbes)

Alexander Dennis Enviro 300 SP58BZE (27551) looks like it is going to be a very busy bus as the shoppers begin to head for home on a very wet summer's day during June 2009. The Enviro 300 series has turned into one of the main bus types used by Stagecoach and is a good, mid-range vehicle for inter-urban work. (*Barry Sanjana*)

Jonckheere Mistral-bodied Volvo B10M V906DPN (52656) is typical of the type of coach to be found on express services the length and breadth of the country. This particular vehicle was new to East Kent buses in 1999 and found its way north thanks to in-house bus movements within the Stagecoach Group. It is now to be found running in normal Stagecoach 'Whoosh' livery. (*Barry Sanjana*)

As well as the Enviro 300, the other main bus type in use with Stagecoach is the Alexander Dennis-bodied MAN 18.24. This one, SP08DBZ (22565), is at one of the High Street stops outside the Primark building, with a healthy load ready to be taken home on service 13A. This bus has 'Tayway' branding and is used on the corridor connecting Monifieth, the city centre, Ninewells and the Technology Park. (*Barry Sanjana*)

Acknowledgements

Once again, I am indebted to the following people for allowing me to use their fantastic images as an aid to illustrating this book or for verifying or providing information on locations and so forth. Without them, the rich variety of images would not exist and would make for some dull and un-interesting reading. In no particular order, my heartfelt thanks go to Paul Redmond; Mike Penn; Dr George Fairbairn; Len Wright; Stephen Dowle; Clive A. Brown; Barry Sanjana; Iain Farquhar; Derek Simpson; Iain Lawson; Neale Elder; Davie Stewart; Gary Seamarks; Suzy Scott; Chris Forbes; and Bill McInroy.